Clinical 5S
for Healthcare

Clinical 5S
for Healthcare

Akio Takahara

For Academic and Quantity Discounts Contact Enna Toll Free: 866-249-7348 or email info@enna.com

Address all comments and inquiries to:

Enna Products Corporation
1602 Carolina St.
Unit B3
Bellingham, WA 98229
Telephone: (360) 306-5369
Fax: (905) 481-0756
E-mail: info@enna.com

Printed in the United States of America

Library of Congress Control Number: 2010926152

Library of Congress Cataloging-in-Publication Data
Takahara, Akio
Clinical 5S
Includes index.
ISBN 978-1-926537-19-1
1. Healthcare Issues (HEA028000)
2. Operations Managment (BUS049000)
3. Organizational Development (BUS103000)

Written by Akio Takahara

English translation by Junpei Nakamuro
Cover by Nicholas Miller
Editor Collin McLoughlin
Associate Editor Shawna Gilleland

Advanced Praise for Clinical 5S

"For those of you who are experiencing difficulties in running operations, are seriously engaged in the reduction of accidents, or who still wonder how best to implement 5S, Akio Takahara has created a unique, straightforward approach. *Clinical 5S for Healthcare* is an invaluable guide that is applicable in all healthcare situations."

- Dennis Gawlik, Director of Purchasing Services
  University of Washington

"It's very refreshing to see a book like this focused on Healthcare – there is tremendous opportunity for improvement in patient experience as well as in reducing medical errors. I recommend this book for any Lean practitioner in Healthcare or any Lean practitioner in any field. A great read and I learned a lot from it."

- Pete Abilla, Lean Blogger
  shmula.com

"Takahara weaves together conceptual and principle based discussions with the results of clinical case studies. The concepts and principles of Clinical 5S are exactingly described to good effect. The case studies include not only successes and failures from which to learn but also helpful examples of forms and processes applied successfully by the institutions."

- Patrick Hagan, President, Chief Operating Officer
  Seattle Children's Hospital

"Clinical 5S for Healthcare is one of the first books that explicitly ties 5S methodology and patient safety principles together. Takahara reinforces leadership accountability for the success of 5S, and the role a 5S program can play in developing leadership skills across the organization. The combination of theory and practical application makes the book very approachable and practical for those just getting started in their 5S efforts, as well as those who are looking for ways to strengthen their 5S efforts."

- Cara Bailey, VP of Continuous Performance Improvement
  Seattle Children's Hospital

Read more at www.enna.com/Clinical5S

**For Academic and Quantity Discounts Contact Enna
Toll Free: 866-249-7348 or email info@enna.com**

CONTENTS

CHAPTER 13   169

LOOKING INTO THE FUTURE

FOREWORD

A GROWING NUMBER OF HOSPITALS AND other healthcare organizations have been actively implementing 5S and other lean methods over the past decade, in North America and around the world.

I have been a part of many 5S efforts and have seen first-hand how 5S empowers healthcare professionals to create a workplace that works better for them, allowing them to provide better patient care. 5S leads to improved quality, patient safety, efficiency, and employee morale. I am passionate about 5S not because I love putting tape outlines around items; I believe in the power of 5S because, with the right mindset, it can unleash a wave of meaningful patient-centered improvements.

5S APPLIES TO HEALTHCARE

It can be easy for healthcare leaders and professionals to discount 5S as a simple tool for factories. Hospital staff might complain that hospitals are far more complex and their work is far more important than anything in a factory — but this is exactly the reason why healthcare needs 5S.

Healthcare organizations and workplaces are full of unnecessary waste – this waste leads to high costs, poor quality, and frustrated professionals. It is fair to assume, and not an exaggeration to say, that a typical hospital has frequent near-misses, or instances of actual patient harm, due to a simple lack of organization. Medications are mistaken for others, supplies are not available in Rapid Response Team carts, and needed equipment is often stored inconveniently far from the point of use. Mr. Takahara illustrates the importance of utilizing 5S to eliminate these wastes and reduce medical malpractices through the case study of Patient N. Though the case study highlights a fatal error that was made by the medical staff, he breaks down the necessary strategies and steps that can be taken to prevent future occurrences in an easy to understand table.

One core 5S principle is to keep the most frequently used equipment close to where it's used — to minimize the time staff members spend walking to retrieve the equipment and encouraging its proper use. In one hospital, managers posted signs lecturing the nurses and techs about the need to use proper lift assist equipment for morbidly obese patients – for the safety of the staff and the patient.

When asked why they might not use the assist, staff members on the 2nd floor unit answered "because it's stored upstairs on the 3rd floor, it's too hard to get to, so we do without." The supply room on the 2nd floor was jammed full of old, broken equipment that wasn't needed or wasn't used as often. An initial 5S initiative helped free up space so the lift assist could be stored on the 2nd floor — eliminating the need for the signs and the management lectures about doing the right thing.

With 5S, we can shift the culture from one where people are blamed for not following management mandates to one where employees are properly supported and treated with respect.

5S IS A MINDSET, NOT A SIMPLE TOOL

When learning about 5S, some hospital employees might say, "Oh yeah, that makes sense — we already label where things go. Our department already looks good." Labeling where items go is just one small part of the 5S methodology. 5S is much more than a one-time "spring cleaning" to make things look neat and tidy.

5S is a mindset and an ongoing approach that supports healthcare professionals so they can provide better patient care. A hospital and leadership team with the 5S mindset creates an environment where staff can take control of their own workplace—empowering people and providing the assistance required to establish, maintain, and continuously improve the workplace. Mr. Takahara provides examples of how the reader can foster this organization-wide mindset of continuous improvement and help draw out the motivation in each staff member to want to continuously improve their workplace.

One nurse, upon touring an excellent lean factory, was struck by the contrast between the factory and her hospital. After seeing visible evidence of 5S and, more importantly, hearing team members describe how they were supported by supervisors and leaders, the nurse commented, "I used to think factories were simple, but I'm blown away by how much care and energy goes into supporting the front-line team members—making sure what they have what they need to do high quality work. They aren't searching and running around looking for tools and parts—they are supported by a system that's designed to make their work easier. I wish we were supported as well in our unit [at the hospital]!"

By touring the factory, the nurse was able to explain to her leaders that they needed to use 5S principles to redesign their space and their support systems—it was much more than a "throw out the junk" activity. 5S is one manifestation of the Toyota guiding principle of "respect for humanity." One of the case studies in this book illustrates an example of the importance of visiting a 5Sed facility in the form of a lean team leader's struggle instilling the need to implement 5S in his employees. By being encouraged to tour a factory that had been successfully implementing 5S for years he gained insights from both the workers and management, which enhanced his own understanding of how to work with people to achieve Clinical 5S. Because he was able to tour successful facilities he was able to internalize and utilize this new knowledge to assist his employees and implement a successful 5S program.

5S CAN IMPROVE PATIENT SAFETY AND QUALITY

5S often gets misrepresented as being merely a method for straightening up the workplace or for making things look good. Or, 5S is describing merely as a way of increasing staff productivity since they do not waste as much time walking to get supplies or searching for needed equipment.

Actually, the 5S mindset and methodology can (and, more importantly, should) have a major impact on clinical quality and patient safety. For example, before lean it might be too time consuming for nurses to gather all of the supplies that are needed to insert a central line in the safest way possible (the way that prevents infections). In an environment full of waste where clinicians are pressured for time, it can be tempting to cut corners and not run back to the supply cabinet that one last time for the additional drape. In a 5S environment, we make it easy for a nurse to quickly gather all items in one trip – making it harder to forget a critical item, eliminating the temptation or need to cut corners.

In one hospital I worked with, there was a near-miss incident that illustrated the need for proper 5S to the staff in a radiology department. During an MRI scan, a young patient became ill and started vomiting. The MRI tech stopped the scan and went into the room to assist the patient. She reached into a cluttered supply bin, where items were haphazardly piled. The tech could not find the suction tube required to clear the patient's mouth and airway.

The tech ran out of the room to the electronic inventory cabinet to get suction tubes and, again, they were not found where they were supposed to be. Even with a high-tech cabinet, the process for re-stocking supplies was not sufficient. The tech ran into another MRI room, interrupting another patient's procedure, to get the needed tubes.

The patient was OK; no harm was done. But the incident, and the story, was used widely in the department to illustrate the need for 5S—making sure the right supplies are always available in the right quantity in the right place. The team moved away from piling supplies into a cabinet (which did not allow for visual control of the inventory levels) and installed more hooks on the wall, where each item would have its own clearly defined place. As part of the pre-procedure checklist, the team could do a visual scan to make sure everything was in place on the wall before the procedure, simply and proactively preventing a similar near-miss from occurring again.

This example and this application of 5S inspired more staff action and patient-focused improvement than a simple effort to organize desk drawers in the control room would have inspired. The book has numerous illustrations and photos to help drive home the points illustrated in the book and give the reader a multitude of ideas for implementing Clinical 5S in their own workplace.

5S IS A FOUNDATION FOR BROADER LEAN THINKING

5S is a popular "starting point" for lean, both in factories and in hospitals. Healthcare organizations can achieve early "quick wins" using 5S, gaining support for further lean efforts. 5S is a good way to test leaders' ability to implement and sustain change. But, care must be taken that lean is not limited to being just a "5S initiative."

5S is an important foundation of lean and should be used as a springboard for an organization to start down the path of their lean journey. 5S helps get employees into a mindset of change, and is something which they can physically see and respond to. The momentum of this mind set then paves the way for future improvements. 5S should serve as an introduction for leaders to learn more about lean—the management system and cultural transformation that is the hallmark of the world's most successful lean healthcare transformations, such as ThedaCare, Virginia Mason Medical Center, Seattle Children's Hospital, and others.

If you start your lean journey with 5S, you will quickly discover opportunities for other lean methods, including standardized work, visual management, and kanban. In fact, if done properly, it's hard to separate these methods are so interconnected in a systemic and systematic approach to lean.

LEARNING TO THINK, NOT JUST COPYING

This book highlights all of the points I have tried to make here. There are many examples, pictures, and guidelines shared with the reader. My advice is that the reader should learn from these examples, and collaborate with their co-workers, employees, and all other staff in order to adapt and create a 5S program that is ideal for their organization. It is important to resist the old "command-and-control" urge of leaders to tell their employees exactly what to do. Top-down mandates about "doing 5S" are not the true spirit of lean or 5S. Read this book for education and inspiration toward a greater understanding of these methods.

It is important to think about "why" these methods are needed, not just "how" to do them. Chapter 3 highlights the "why's" of Clinical 5S, and each of the "S's" are broken down into individual chapters within the book for easy reference. If you, the reader, feel you have hit a stumbling block or lost direction during implementation then open up Clinical 5S again to help energize and bring you back on track. Bringing a greater understanding of these concepts into the workplace, with the assistance of books such as Clinical 5S, will start your healthcare organization on a path to profound lean thinking, not just implementing 5S.

Mark Graban

Award winning author of *Lean Hospitals: Improving Quality, Patient Safety, and Employee Satisfaction*

A Note from the Publisher

TODAY I FEEL VERY PRIVILEGED to provide you with this unique and comprehensive book, which has greatly benefited many healthcare organizations across Japan. I have been leading up to the discovery of this book for the last 36 years and today, on my birthday, I feel fortunate to be writing the publisher's foreword.

On June 10, 1975 our family life changed in an instant due to a motor vehicle accident that led to my father becoming a paraplegic for life. I would not come to understand the implications of this until I began experiencing, first hand, the struggles healthcare organizations have with delivering quality care in a manner that provides value to the patient. Though this is not a new struggle, it has most recently been the center of the media and political spotlight.

Dominating the media daily is talk about a medical crisis in this country. In the 1970's the United States only spent 7% of its GDP on healthcare whereas today it is estimated to be above 16% of GDP, the second highest among all United Nations member nations. The Health and Human Services Department expects that the health share of GDP will continue its historical upward trend, reaching 19.5% of GDP by 2017.

What we fail to realize is that the crisis was always there, it was simply hidden because the population was so young that it did not reveal the entire cost. Since the US population was so young in the 1970's most of the population only required minor procedures, with few complications and rapid recovery times, which benefited the system. Now that same population, 36 years later, is requiring systemic care as they age, which exaggerates the numerous imperfections in the system. It is these imperfections which need to be dealt with in order to increase the quality of care and reduce the costs associated with healthcare.

If I look back on why I looked for a book like this and other gems of wisdom in Japan, it began after a participant on our Study Mission to Japan, Alice Lee of Beth Israel Deaconess Medical Center, began talking about the challenges and similarities between healthcare and other industries. She was impressed by the similarities and challenges of managing resources, people, machines, information, and delivering quality services that we witnessed in other industries. In our discussions I realized the true extent of the similarity of challenges between healthcare and other industries, and that great methodologies transcend both industry and profession.

Over the years my family has not been alone in their dissatisfaction with the healthcare industry, and even the people within the industry are not satisfied with their organization's performance. This collection of experiences inspires me to become more involved in improving the industry, and I believe this book will contribute to a more systematic improvement of the methodologies within the healthcare industry.

Mr. Takahara is the foremost expert on 5S in healthcare and he developed his Clinical 5S program to assist hospitals and other medical facilities in reducing their waste and clutter, virtually eliminating the human errors which plague most healthcare facilities today, and creating a more positive and enjoyable place to work and visit.

Though Lean and the tools of Lean in healthcare have recently been discussed in great depth, it is difficult to find methodologies that are specialized for healthcare and are applicable to, and achievable for, every staff member at every level of an organization. It is commonly understood that in order to remain at the top of one's field, one needs to change, grow, and expand their knowledge continuously. Clinical 5S for Healthcare will assist healthcare professionals in achieving these objectives.

This book not only focuses on the implication of demographic trends in the healthcare system, but also considers the ability to deliver the best healthcare, at the fastest possible speed, in the most economical manner, and still improve the quality of care. As an industry, we need to focus on the value and eliminate the natural wastes in the system by establishing world-class methodologies.

As the healthcare industry strives for positive change, I am proud to offer this source for discussion, inspiration, and innovation.

Collin McLoughlin
President, Enna

PREFACE

"Sort," "Set in Order," "Shine," "Standardize," and "Sustain"

ACCIDENTS IN HOSPITALS HAVE BEEN recognized as a serious societal problem. We all know that patients bring themselves to hospitals for the purpose of receiving appropriate medical attention, however there have been many instances where the conditions of such patients has worsened during the course of receiving treatment by being thrown into medical malpractices. In some extreme cases, we are confronted by the news that a patient has been disabled or even killed by such medical mistreatments.

An increasing number of hospitals are experiencing difficulties running their business. As the nation of Japan tackles the serious challenge of reducing the rising medical cost that is to be paid by Japan's universal healthcare system, the expected revenue for hospitals has been drastically cut down. Given this current situation, discovering ways to cut the operating costs of hospitals by the elimination of wastes, by any possible method, is the most significant challenge they face.

There are many leading causes for medical accidents. One prominent factor is the overall workplace environment of hospitals. Some examples of accident-causing factors are miscommunication, the wrong administration of medicines, and patients falling. These factors are closely related to existing issues about how work is performed and how workplaces within the hospital environment are organized. From the point of view of hospital management in promoting continuous improvement, excess amounts of medical equipment and furniture, found in many modern hospitals, need to be eliminated because they are simply waste.

In fact, there are many case studies where the number of medical errors are significantly reduced, and wastes are eliminated, simply by changing how each task is performed within a workplace. The "5S activities" derived from manufacturing are responsible for such drastic improvements. The 5S activities require the full-participation of every worker within an organization and enforce the following concepts: "Sort," "Set in Order," "Shine," "Standardize," and "Sustain."

This book introduces you to the philosophies behind the application of the proven effectiveness of 5S in the manufacturing fields as they relate to the hospital environment, as well as being a practical guide as to how it can be successfully implemented in the clinical environment. The concepts of 5S are described in depth in this book by providing you with actual implementation case studies from successful hospitals. Even though it is usually hard to quantify the level of benefits returned by it, 5S definitely leads to a promotion of changes in the consciousness among nurses and other staff members by eliminating even the slightest possibility for medical accidents through a comprehensive elimination of waste in their work environment.

In addition, the 5S activities are bound to trigger changes in the organizational cultures in which hospitals operate. Hospitals, as organizational entities, are institutions that consist of various experts coming together from different fields of study. They are doctors, nurses, pharmacists, technicians, nutritionists, and so on. With such a varied group of experts all in one place, everyone tends to mind his or her own business and is reluctant to work outside of their comfort zone. Such an organizational culture discourages necessary communication from taking place and threatens any coordination among the different departments, especially when inter-departmental duties need be performed in a timely manner. Everyone knows that medical care ought to be based upon internal teamwork, however many medical professionals today face the challenge of promoting such a mentality of teamwork in the first place.

Interesting results were discovered when the 5S activities were introduced to such unorganized hospital working environments. Many hospitals that were lacking in interdepartmental coordination suffered from delays in implementing 5S, meaning that such workplaces were lacking a commitment toward promoting continuous improvement. The fact that a proper management structure to facilitate the changes failed to be established became very apparent.

5S tolerates no excuses and makes it clear whether organizations are committed to acquiring continuous improvement or not. After ensuring their dedication to practicing Kaizen, organizations will begin to experience the true and tangible benefits of 5S and their organizational culture will be reformed in such a way as to accommodate changes for improvement.

However, upon the implementation of 5S in hospital environments there is absolutely no guarantee that medical accidents and wastes can be completely eliminated. It is often apparent that accidents still occur because 5S is not enforced in a thorough manner. Holding an excess amount of wasteful inventory is another consequence of inconsistent implementation of the 5S activities. My point is that the 5S activities do not stop medical accidents automatically but are one of the significant prerequisites for achieving that goal. Moreover, 5S is a fundamental tool for carrying out work, and this foundation must be set in place with great attention to detail.

The first half of this book is designed to explain the true meaning of, and practical methodologies for, 5S implementation, with a focus on the principles that are essential for the development of 5S in a hospital environment. The second half of the book illustrates a series of case studies of actual 5S implementations that have taken place in Takeda General Hospital (located in Fukushima, Japan). I would like you to understand the principles and then analyze the implementation examples so that you will have a true grasp of effective 5S application techniques.

In addition, the structure and content of this book is customized so that you will be able to use the information provided and case studies as an implementation manual for your own organization. I hope that this book will help those of you who are striving to energize your workplace and eliminate wastes through establishing a foundation based on the 5S system.

Akio Takahara

ABOUT THE AUTHOR

WHILE DESIGNING PRODUCTION LINES AND implementing a continuous improvement plan for Canon early in his career, Mr. Takahara realized the importance of increasing the strength of management and the need for 5S to be implemented thoroughly in order to ensure positive results. His passion for improving the quality of businesses has continuously increased since then, which has led him to pursue a career in business consulting.

Mr. Takahara's continuously strives to better himself, and this truly comes through in his work. He has continued to earn many degrees and certificates through the Sanno Institute of Management and the All-Japan Federation of Management, Zen-Noh-Ren, which was established in 1949 to bring together all management and consultancies to provide the best training possible to help them succeed. In 1998, Mr. Takahara established his own consulting firm, Basic Management Laboratory, and continues to provide consulting services while maximizing his extensive network within hospitals and corporations across Japan.

Though he began his journey into Lean through various industries, Mr. Takahara's strongest interest has emerged in the field of healthcare. Creating a safer, healthier, less stressful, and less wasteful environment increases the happiness and productivity of everyone involved. He has assisted numerous hospitals and clinics in the successful implementation of 5S, greatly reducing the number of medical accidents and wasteful activities prevalent in their facilities.

The following are some of the hospitals in Japan which he has been an integral part of leading the way for thorough 5S implementation.

- Takeda General Hospital
- Iwata City Hospital
- Ogikubo Hospital
- Hokuriku Central Hospital

Each hospital above has succeeded in adapting 5S thoroughly, and with the complete support of the staff. As a result, their workplace culture has transformed positively and every staff member is actively participating in continuous improvement activities. These hospitals will continue to thrive in the ever changing healthcare environment because they have a solid foundation in place and each new staff member is trained and encouraged to participate in 5S practices.

Mr. Takahara has also worked with more than 20 medical institutions as a guest speaker or workshop facilitator. A few of these institutes include Kyoto University Hospital, Tokai University Hachioji Hospital, and Kitazato University Hospital. Mr. Takahara teaches the 'Basic Action Requirements', each workers daily responsibilities, which are essential for ensuring a company's long-term success, the improvement of workers' problem-solving abilities, and cultivating workers who are able to create and designate their own roles within an organizational setting. He unwaveringly believes that by teaching companies to focus on their employees as the most valuable resource the company itself will change for the better and create and environment where each person holds themselves responsible for change and actively pursues a better working environment.

Following the 5S transformation of Takeda General Hospital, Mr. Takahara was requested by the Japan Medical Associates to publish a book, which is titled "Correspondence Education for Medical Safety". After completing the requested work, he began writing Clinical 5S.

66 *As it remains a serious challenge to completely eliminate the root cause of medical errors from operations, I sincerely believe that implementation of Clinical 5S is the most significant starting point for preventing medical malpractices from occurring.* 99

  - Akio Takahara

CHAPTER 1
HOSPITALS AND 5S

1-1 CHALLENGES THAT HOSPITALS FACE
CHRONIC OCCURRENCE OF HOSPITAL ACCIDENTS

THE CHALLENGES THAT HOSPITALS FACE nowadays are overwhelming. One of the most critical issues found in hospitals is a chronic occurrence of accidents, which has recently been getting a lot of attention, as it has become a societal problem. Accidents in hospitals should not happen at all, but the fact is accidents are frequent and are happening continuously in hospital settings.

According to a research study conducted by the Japanese Ministry of Internal Affairs and Communication (MIAC), the same types of accidents are occurring in large-scale hospitals across Japan. In order to find out more about the cause of frequent accidents, the MIAC decided to carry out a nationwide survey. Among both regular and private medical facilities in Japan, 217 facilities were chosen and accidents that had occurred

1

from January 2001 through July, 2002 (a year and half) were studied extensively.

According to the results, the same major types of accidents had occurred at the rate of 91 cases in 17 facilities during this time period. Such accidents included those involving leaving surgical instruments or gauze in patient's bodies and administering inaccurate doses of I.V.

For instance, a few years ago in K. University Hospital, a patient who had just gone through an operation for joint rheumatism at 9AM was supposed to receive antibiotics and an I.V. of Heparin Saline, to prevent blood coagulation. Instead, the patient ended up dying because she was given an I.V. of antiseptic solution called "Chlorhexidine Gluconate," which was supposed to be administered to another patient. Many factors can be considered the cause of this accident, however I believe that the lack of 5S was one of the prominent reasons why this accident happened.

EXISTENCE OF WASTE IN MANAGEMENT

Another problem is the presence of hidden wastes within hospital administration. As you already know, most hospitals have been suffering from deficit balances. One of the main reasons for this is that the administrative sector of hospitals are usually filled with more wastes than general companies are. Of course, hospitals have confronted many other serious systematic issues with national healthcare plans and revised medical treatment fees, however, I am going to concentrate my effort on analyzing various wastes associated with how work is being performed within the organizational structure of hospitals.

Many categories of wastes can be discovered in hospitals. Performing unnecessary work in hospital operations and conducting unnecessary treatments, from the point of view of patients, are the most prominent categories of waste found. Most of such wastes can be eliminated by implementing extensive continuous improvement practices, such as a thorough use of the 5S's.

For instance, nurse stations in general tend to hold an excess amount of inventory due to a lack of proper stock management. If inventories are not consumed right away it not only clutters their office spaces but it also hides the financial investment that has been made in the unused inventory. From a management perspective this is a huge waste. What is needed is to supply only the necessary items, in necessary quantities, at the right time (Just-in-Time).

What was just described is only one example. Certain hospitals, often without knowing it, are suffering from the types of wastes that are unimaginable to factories and general companies, therefore it goes without saying that a higher level of 5S implementation in such hospitals is premature. I strongly believe that the management techniques which have been proven to be effective in factory settings can be applied to improve these situations, and that 5S can establish a solid foundation to solve many other serious issues.

1-2 MEDICAL ACCIDENTS AND THE 5S'S

1-2-1 MEDICAL ACCIDENTS AND HUMAN ERROR

In this section, let us examine the relationship between medical errors and the main theme of this book, 5S. There are many causing factors for medical accidents. It is indicated that the main trigger for medical accidents is strongly related to misunderstandings by humans; in another words, human errors. The secret to preventing medical accidents is to eliminate human errors in any way possible. First, let us analyze what human errors are all about.

GENERAL DEFINITION OF "HUMAN ERROR"

"Human error" can be defined in the following ways:

"The decisions or activities of humans that hurt, damage, and discourage the functionality, safety, efficiency, comfort, profit, intention, and emotion of other human beings, animals, items, systems, and the natural environment."

> — Defined by Shigeru Hage, Professor at Rikkyo
>   University, Dept. of Literature.

"Human error is caused by the gap between the level of expected ability of humans and what can actually be achieved by humans. Consequently, this gap leads to human malfunctions that have the potential to negatively impact the system, in one way or another."

> — Defined by Hiroshi Tamura, Professor at Hiroshima International University, Department of Human and Environment Studies.

"'Error' is a failure caused by our inability to carry out activities as planned, and our wrong decision-making process in formulating strategies to achieve desired results."

> — Defined by an American healthcare institution.

Definition of "Human Error" by the Author

I will define the term "human error," as used in this book, as follows:

> "Human error is essentially a human malfunction that occurs in the process of understanding, decision-making, and carrying out an action. Humans continue to suffer from such failures no matter how much attention is given to trying to not make any mistakes. "

An important point in my definition is that humans are always inclined to fail and make mistakes, even though they are doing their best not to do so. We must remember in analyzing human errors that "it is human nature to make mistakes," and appropriate solutions and continuous improvement ideas must be generated with this truth in mind at all times.

1-2-2 Causes of Human Error

Developmental phases of human error

Let us analyze an occurrence of human error by applying it to the process of human activities. Developmental stages of human error are:

Phase 1: Current Situation Recognition Stage

Phase 2: Assessment and Decision-Making Stage

Phase 3: Action Stage

(refer to Figure 1.1)

In the first phase, errors occur in the process of acknowledging the current situation. Insufficient collection and misinterpretation of facts leads to errors. In other words, when faced with a new environment from which information needs to be collected, humans often have an inaccurate perception of the truth by a misunderstanding, preconceived notion, and/or subconscious reaction to the problem.

For instance, a local newspaper once reported a serious medical accident where a patient was forced into a coma because a wrong medicine, called "Amaryl," was prescribed instead of the correct medicine, called "Almarl." As you can see, both names are extremely similar and the wrong medicine was dispatched to the patient because its name resembled that of the correct medicine.

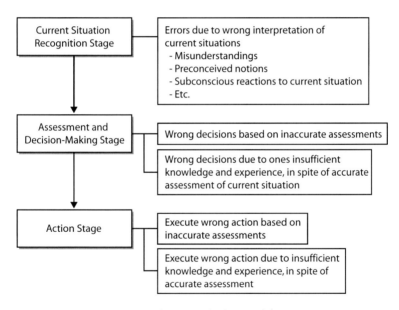

Figure 1.1 Developmental Phases of Human Error

In the second phase, errors are caused in the stage of making assessments and decisions. Wrong decisions are carried out based upon inaccurate assessments. Even when an assessment of facts is accurate errors can still occur due to insufficient levels of knowledge and experience in making correct decisions. In addition, one's misunderstandings and biases can also have a significant influence on whether or not the right decision can be made.

For instance, in a case of setting an accurate speed of I.V. drip errors can be made by performing a wrong calculation or misreading a reference chart, even if one completely understands the logic behind how the rate of drip must be calculated.

In the final phase, errors occur in the process of action. Wrong actions can be carried out based on both accurate and inaccurate assessments. This phase explains the fact that errors are caused due to the lack of experience and the technique of a given individual. This applies to doctors and nurses, who make critical mistakes due to lack of experience and unpracticed techniques.

WHAT IS AN ASSUMPTION?

Humans do not perceive their reality solely based on facts collected objectively, but are able to speculate risks even in an unprecedented situation by applying their past experiences and knowledge to whatever the situation brings. Then, based on such predictions and preconceived notions, we carry out an action with a certain pattern of tendencies.

An assumption is the result of the lack of using a decision-making process. In addition, such factors as a habitual reaction to problems, resistance to change in management by supervisors, and overconfidence in one's actions often lead to an assumption. There are many cases where an assumption originates from a misunderstanding. As humans cannot be completely free from having misunderstandings, the most important thing is to recognize the fact that misunderstandings are constantly happening, in one way or another. However, in reality when an assumption becomes personally embedded into one's beliefs, often one's assumptions go unnoticed unless the situation becomes too destructive because of it, which is often too late.

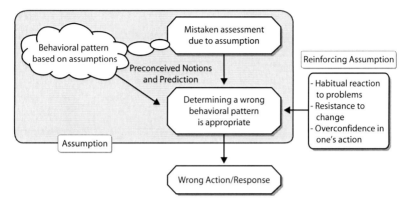

Figure 1.2 What is an Assumption?

How to reduce misperception

Misperception can be described in a situation where A is wrongly perceived as B. If this mistake can be corrected right away then serious consequences can be avoided. However, assuming the accuracy of one's understanding always leads to a serious outcome in the end.

So why do humans perceive reality inaccurately? There are many factors to explain that. Typical reasons for that are as follows.

A misunderstanding is made because:

- A & B look similar to one another
- It has been a common practice to identify A as B by mistake, therefore one continues to make the same error
- One forgets previous actions or preventative measures and continues to act as they have in the past
- One decides to make their own personal judgment in an ambiguous situation or setting

One of the common factors in these reasons is that humans have plenty of leeway to make their own assumptions, as there are no rules in place to ensure that humans follow a certain checklist to produce accurate judgments. In other words, on a premise that humans always make errors in perceiving reality it is extremely important to create an environment where critical information for decision-making can be clearly visualized so that the slightest potential for a mistake can be completely eliminated in the first place.

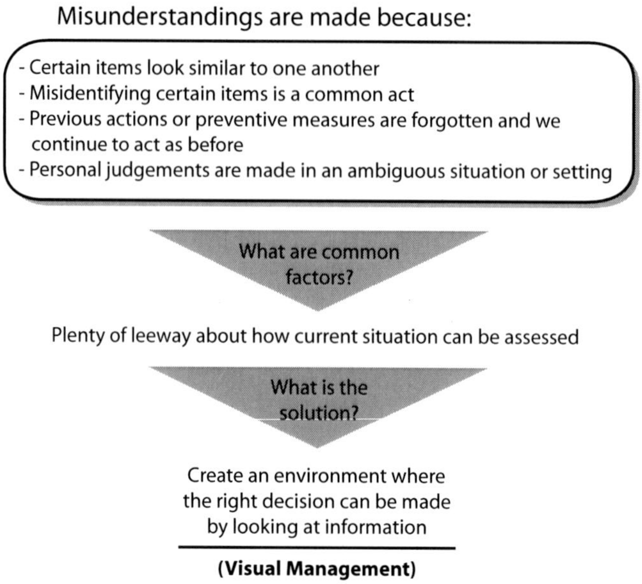

Misunderstandings are made because:

- Certain items look similar to one another
- Misidentifying certain items is a common act
- Previous actions or preventive measures are forgotten and we continue to act as before
- Personal judgements are made in an ambiguous situation or setting

What are common factors?

Plenty of leeway about how current situation can be assessed

What is the solution?

Create an environment where the right decision can be made by looking at information

(Visual Management)

Figure 1.3 How to Remove Assumption and Misunderstanding

PREVENT UNINTENTIONALLY-GENERATED ACTIONS

A widely implemented solution, designed to avoid unconscious actions, is the "Point & Call" activity. In this activity people pay extra attention to detail by going through a checklist and making sure that every item is clearly in place by pointing at the actual items while vocalizing their names out loud.

The "Point & Call" activity effectively converts unconscious activities into conscious activities by making humans pay attention to specifics and creating an environment where such critical checklist information can be shared among everyone. By establishing appropriate Visual Management systems we are able to create an error proof workplace with a high degree of effectiveness.

1-2-3 A WORKPLACE THAT GENERATES HUMAN ERRORS

Human errors occur as the results of misperception, preconceived notions, and activities that take place in the unconscious state of mind. These are indeed the weaknesses of human beings. We must acknowledge that not only are humans responsible for making errors but also that it is a human's natural tendency to make the error.

When a human error occurs, whoever caused the error is often blamed by others and goes through serious scrutiny. However, it is not the fault of the person responsible for the error, rather it is the fault of the work environment for allowing even the slightest room for such an error to occur in the first place. Therefore the workplace must be designed to become error-proof, given the premise that "humans always make mistakes, no matter how hard we attempt not to." For instance, if an error occurs due to misperception, the responsible human is not to be blamed. Instead the work environment ought to be questioned for allowing humans to make a mistake of any sort. We must also look at it as problematic if such a workplace is never continuously improved, leaving the root cause of a problem untouched.

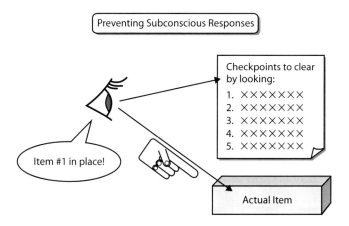

Figure 1.4 Preventing Subconscious Responses

1-2-4 IMPLEMENTING THE 5S'S TO ELIMINATE THE ROOT CAUSE OF AN ERROR

The most important approach to preventing the occurrence of medical accidents is by terminating every contributing factor in a thorough fashion. Given the fact that a wide range of error causing factors exist in a hospital environment it is most effective, and should be a minimum hospital requirement, to concentrate efforts upon improving the working organization for the purpose of eliminating errors that are based upon human misperception and preconceived notions.

CHAPTER 2
THE 5S ACTIVITIES IN HOSPITALS

2-1 PHILOSOPHY BEHIND AND EFFECTIVENESS OF THE 5S ACTIVITIES

PRINCIPLES OF THE 5S ACTIVITIES

THE MEANING OF IMPLEMENTING 5S is as follows:

The 5S activities introduced to organizations, information systems, and people, are the 5 main principles, "Sort," "Set in Order," "Shine," "Standardize," and "Sustain," require the full participation of the affected community. It is designed to establish a basic organizational structure that promotes operational efficiency, elimination of human errors and accidents, and efficient usage of overall work space. Moreover, the 5S activities are most likely to reinforce a supervisor's management capacities through a vitalization of the workplace.

The following principles are important elements in the implementation of 5S:

1. Targets of 5S are goods, information, and people.

   5S is applied to goods, information, and people. For goods and information, 4S ("Sort," "Set in Order," "Shine, and "Standardize") is mainly intended. As far as 5S for people is concerned, the principle of "Sustain" comes into effect. A great deal of positive results can be expected from Sorting and Setting goods in Order, but the implementation of the "Sustain" principle is indispensable in order to yield expected results of 5S in the long run.

2. Full participation is required.

   5S requires an atmosphere filled with enthusiasm and the commitment of the workforce and should be viewed as an important organizational goal that concerns each member of the team. "Full participation" and "leadership role" are the key elements for achieving this type of workplace culture. "Leadership role" is not just for leaders to achieve but is also for everyone else who chooses responsible behaviors that are worth the rest of the team following. Management supervisors and 5S team leaders, especially, must set good examples for their team members to keep them on track with the program. Unless they are able to do so, the team members often get turned off and full 5S participation will fail to be accomplished.

3. 5S builds the foundation for yielding various continuous improvement results.

   Implementation of 5S is expected to contribute not only to directly eliminating wastes and preventing errors from occurring, but also to establishing the basic foundation for continuous improvement. In organizations where 5S is inadequately in place, the results of any continuous improvement efforts often remain unseen due to the lack of a foundation.

4. Aim for vitalization of the organization and improving the management skills of supervisors by implementing 5S.

   It is important to bring about improvements in supervisor's management skills and energize the workplace as a whole by implementing 5S. A direct benefit of 5S is the elimination of waste by continuous improvement. An indirect benefit of 5S is an improvement of the level of management within the entire organization.

CHARACTERISTICS OF 5S

5S demands the full participation of everyone, as well as being designated the standard work routine. Characteristics of 5S that have been implemented in general corporations are as follows:

1. 5S is performing work as it should be performed.

   It should be easy to perform work as it is supposed to be performed, however in reality it is quite challenging to actually do so. For instance, one should always be able to greet other people, put items back where they belong after use, be on time, follow guidelines, and keep promises. However, it is extremely difficult to be able to achieve these, which are considered to be simple tasks, in a predetermined way in organizational settings.

2. The degree of 5S implementation determines the management strength of the organization.

   The level of thoroughness of 5S in an organization reflects upon the effectiveness of supervisor's management skills. A certain level of management strength is required so that rules will be followed, in a predetermined manner, in order to accomplish tasks, as well as comply with specific timelines. Once again, what is considered a commonsensical task seems easy to accomplish, but in reality is extremely challenging for us to sustain.

3. The level of 5S thoroughness determines a person's sense of morale toward their workplace.

   Morale can be translated into one's feeling of belonging to the corporate culture and workplace environment. Such a feeling among staff members has a tremendous influence upon how well 5S can be implemented. In other words, a workplace where the level of 5S implementation is quite high will often have a high degree of motivation and dedication in its members toward their work. Satisfaction with work and the work environment among staff members is an element in a successful implementation 5S.

4. 5S represents the condition of management in a workplace.

The level of 5S implementation represents the quality of management in a workplace. It is indicated that the Sorting and Setting in Order of information are important prerequisites to managing a workplace effectively. Management by sight, such as being able to retrieve necessary information quickly and representing information in a clear manner, is essential. We can evaluate the level of management by analyzing how well 5S is implemented.

5. The theories behind 5S are simple and the progress of 5S is easy to evaluate by sight.

The logic of 5S should be simple and easy for everyone to understand. In addition, the level of progress and thoroughness should also be easily understood by sight. These are very important points to cultivate when implementing 5S. The ability to monitor the progress of continuous improvement makes management much easier. It is this ease of management and the ability to understand progress that enforces the thoroughness of 5S implementation. You cannot expect sufficient results out of anything in general by taking tepid approaches. Thoroughness is our ultimate goal.

6. 5S practices should be routine and well established in the workplace.

5S does not present us with its real benefits unless it becomes a routine practice and is integrated well into our daily activities. A short-term use of 5S, as in such a manner as "instantaneous wind speed," does not mean that 5S is administered in the most effective manner. What I mean by "routine" here is how we should become restless and do not feel like ourselves when we do not practice 5S, no matter how cumbersome the activities can be. Thoroughness when implementing 5S can be achieved by falling into a habit of carrying out 5S practices in a continuous manner.

Meaning of 5S in hospitals

Fundamentally speaking, there is no difference between 5S within hospitals and 5S that takes place in factories and other companies. The selection of focus areas and points to remember when administering Clinical 5S, however, greatly varies. Primarily it is how 5S is established as a basic foundation to prevent medical malpractices from occurring and promoting operational efficiency. The implementation of 5S removes various kinds of waste and eliminates the principle factors that can lead to medical accidents.

It is important to energize the workplace and increase customer satisfaction by improving your level of competency in achieving the ideas described above. The level of management strength within the organization plays a significant role in this effort. After all, 5S identifies the quality of organizational management. In other words, the level of 5S implementation does not improve unless there is a high level of management in place to start with.

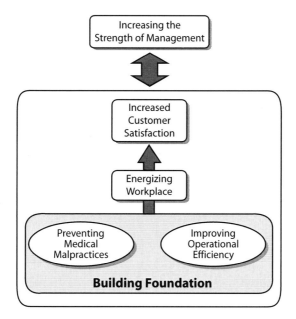

Figure 2.1 The Meaning of 5S in Hospitals

AIM OF 5S ACTIVITIES IN HOSPITALS

From now on, for this book, I will call 5S that is used in the hospital environment "Clinical 5S." The correlation between Clinical 5S and various other management tools are described in Figure 2.2, which also explains the establishment of a fundamental management structure in a hospital environment.

Figure 2.2 Aim of 5S Activities in Hospitals

As you can see, Clinical 5S plays the most critical role, especially in promoting effective Safety Management and Hygiene Control. The truly desired results can be expected only when the essence of management itself is clearly identified and put into practice without fault. Putting management into practice without fault simply means to diligently follow routines and rules that everyone has agreed upon in advance. It is extremely important for every worker to internalize the ability to follow rules through the implementation of Clinical 5S.

Many types of management activities are being promoted not only in hospitals but also in various non-hospital organizations. The basic rules state that certain rules and standard operating procedures must be clearly established first and each member of the team must be following them at all times. In other words, desirable results can never be attained when rules are not followed, no matter how innovative a management system may appear to be. I cannot emphasize more that the habitual practice of following rules is indispensable in order to effectively manage safety in a hospital environment.

Having said that, Clinical 5S can be expected to become a remarkable tool for cultivating an organizational culture where rules are always followed, which becomes an essential foundation for managing a workplace. Many hospitals conduct activities for preventing the occurrence of the medical incidents that can pose some potentially serious medical errors. This is another effective method for eliminating medical malpractices.

It is important to make the situations with a higher potential for medical errors clearly visible; doing so is an effective method of raising an awareness of the issue among workers. However, many workplaces fail to go beyond raising the issue at hand. One of the reasons for this is that they do not possess concrete approaches to solving the problem. Clinical 5S assists the problem solving activities of accident-prone areas of operation and in return leads to many continuous improvement suggestions among employees, as they begin to analyze a workplace from a 5S perspective. In any event, Clinical 5S is the foundation for promoting medical safety and improving operational efficiency. I personally believe that a workplace without Clinical 5S in place is not qualified to talk about medical safety.

2-2 EFFECTIVENESS OF CLINICAL 5S

Let me describe here the expected benefits of implementing Clinical 5S. Generally speaking, people understand 5S as merely cleaning and sorting practices within a workplace. If this were true we would expect hospitals to only be clean by sight. However, we can never expect the true benefits of Clinical 5S if its essential purpose and effectiveness are ignored.

As described in Figure 2.3, there are 2 fundamental benefits in what Clinical 5S can achieve. The first is the direct advantage of Clinical 5S, mainly shown as the elimination of various wastes through implementing Clinical 5S. The second benefit is increased management efficiency. Quality of management improves as the level of Clinical 5S becomes more sophisticated, which is usually the indirect benefit of Clinical 5S implementation.

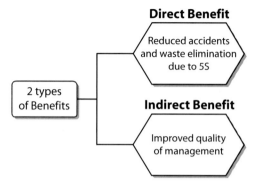

Figure 2.3 Effectiveness of Clinical 5S

DIRECT BENEFITS OF CLINICAL 5S

What I mean here by "direct benefits" are those benefits that contribute to hospital management by directly reducing medical accidents and eliminating operational wastes through Clinical 5S implementation. Some direct benefits of Clinical 5S are as follows:

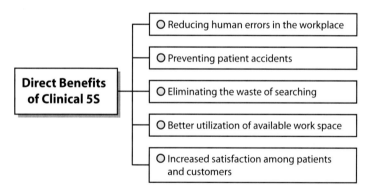

Figure 2.4 Direct Benefits of Clinical 5S

1. Reducing human errors in the workplace.

   Human errors caused by doctors, nurses, and pharmacists are one of the main causes of medical malpractices. Such human errors are usually due to misunderstandings and preconceived notions. A thorough implementation of Clinical 5S establishes a foundation for preventing human errors from occurring, and Visual Management tools play an especially effective role in error proofing.

2. Preventing patient accidents.

There is a higher risk for accidents in an environment where the hallways in a hospital are cluttered with medical equipment. Children, handicapped, and elderly patients can easily become injured by running into these obstacles. Hospitals must require a working environment which anyone could visit with peace of mind. To achieve this it is absolutely necessary to maintain safe passage, identify visual information correctly, and continuously improve areas that are considered unsafe by implementing Clinical 5S.

3. Eliminating the waste of searching.

There is a waste of having to search for items in hospitals. Workers continue to waste their time and energy searching for the right medical charts, medicines, and medical supplies in nurse centers, supply rooms, and pharmacy departments. Most of this need for searching can be eliminated by implementing Clinical 5S in a thorough manner. It is important to understand here not only that these types of searching activities lead to wasteful operation but also that searching eventually leads to the occurrence of medical accidents.

4. Better utilization of available work space.

As you already know, hospitals deal with many different shapes of supplied items, medicines, medical equipment, and documents, and the number of items keeps increasing as medical practices have become more sophisticated over recent years. Relatively older hospital buildings, especially, suffer from lack of space, which results in operations that are difficult to maintain. The implementation of 5S is able to improve such work environments and bring a great deal of value to hospitals by utilizing available space in a much more effective manner.

5. Increased satisfaction among patients and customers.

Satisfaction among patients and customers will drastically increase if the hospital environment is continuously improved with a strong emphasis on creating the impression that anyone can receive necessary treatment safely and comfortably upon visiting the hospital. For example, better hospital environments such as friendly communication between patients and staff, a sense of freshness in the medical ward due to consistent Shining, and a clear indication of signs will be achieved through effectively implementing Clinical 5S.

INDIRECT BENEFITS OF CLINICAL 5S

As I noted before, there are some indirect benefits to management of Clinical 5S in addition to direct benefits. The direct benefits of Clinical 5S are important, however the indirect advantages of Clinical 5S upon management deserve just as much attention. If the management advantages were to be described in one sentence, it would be: "The implementation of Clinical 5S in a comprehensive manner enables supervisors to manage and instruct the fundamental practices performed by every single staff person on his team."

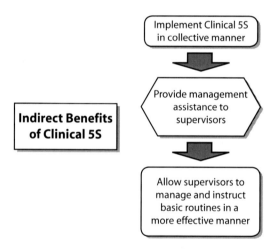

Figure 2.5 Indirect Benefits of Clinical 5S

Establishing a work environment and culture where a hospital collectively implements Clinical 5S together leads to creating motivation among workers to always follow the fundamental rules of operation and standard work procedures. With this type of work culture in place supervisors will be able to instruct and manage workers in following rules at all times. This work environment and culture is absolutely necessary for workers to follow standard work processes and can also lead to the prevention of medical accidents (direct benefit of Clinical 5S).

Chapter 3

Analyzing the Meaning of Clinical 5S

3-1 Definition of Terms in Clinical 5S

The term Clinical 5S is made up of 5 words that start with the letter "S": "Sort" (Seiri), "Set in Order" (Seiton), "Shine" (Seiso), "Standardize" (Seiketsu), and "Sustain" (Shitsuke). Definitions of these terms must be understood clearly in order to convey the true implications of Clinical 5S.

Let me describe the definitions to you. I would like you to memorize the explanations on the following page, if you can.

Term	Definition
Sort (Seiri)	Separate what is necessary from what is unnecessary. Eliminate unnecessary items for good.
Set in Order (Seiton)	Place items a certain way, at a designated location, with clear visual indication in order to find necessary items effortlessly.
Shine (Seiso)	Clean your workplace while conducting inspection.
Standardize (Seiketsu)	Continue practicing "Sort","Set in Order", and "Shine" in a thorough manner and keep a clean environment. Establish Visual Management.
Sustain (Shitsuke)	Put it all into a daily routine in which rules are followed at all times.

Table 3.1 Definitions of Clinical 5S

3-2 RELEVANCY AMONG TERMS WITHIN CLINICAL 5S

It is extremely important to carry out "Sort," "Set in Order," "Shine," and "Standardize" separately. Practice "Sort" first and, after having done that, move on to "Set in Order," then "Shine." Generally, it is understood that "Sort" and "Set in Order" are the same concept, however as far as the implementation of Clinical 5S is concerned, it is critical to separate "Sort" from "Set in Order" and perform them individually. "Standardize" means the condition in which "Sort," "Set in Order," and "Shine" are solidly in place. "Sustain" does not follow any order or sequence—it has to be integrated into each principle at all times.

3-3 WHAT IS "SORT"?
MEANING OF "SORT"

"Sort" simply means separating what is necessary from what is unnecessary and eliminating the unnecessary items once and for all. "Sort" is the most important step to accomplishing an effective adaptation of Clinical 5S. It is safe to say that 5S will never be successful unless "Sort" is accomplished in a thorough manner first. I cannot stress enough that "Sort" is the quintessential principle of Clinical 5S.

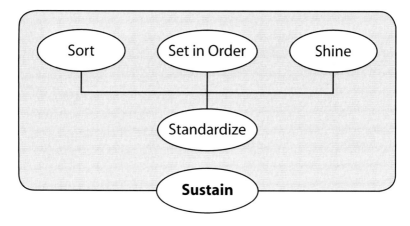

Figure 3.1 Relevancy Among 5S Principles

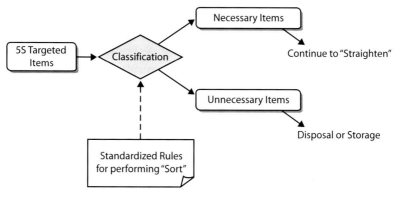

Figure 3.2 Overview of 5S

SEPARATE WHAT IS NECESSARY FROM WHAT IS UNNECESSARY

A certain set of standards must first be set, in order to make judgments on what is necessary and what is unnecessary. It is often extremely difficult to define what is needed and what can be eliminated as unnecessary items. It is because of our inability or unwillingness to make this critical judgment that we continue to leave unnecessary items, such as documents, medicines, medical supplies, and medical devices in our work places. This situation not only leads to the cluttering of a workspace but also makes it difficult to retrieve what is really necessary with little effort and in a timely manner.

THROW AWAY WHAT IS UNNECESSARY

It is important to note that I do not mean throw away everything, simply that we need to eventually get rid of items that we no longer use. However, some items found in your workplace may turn out to be useful to other departments. Such items need to be managed and stored separately. Still, the basic rule of thumb is to throw away what is judged to be unnecessary. Stop thinking that you may need the items sometime in the future and throw them away decisively.

I often hear people giving me an excuse saying, "Sorting is impossible because of the lack of space." They are running out of space because they have not been Sorting their workplace in the past. The important thing to do first is to practice "Sort" throughout the organization and create free space which can then be utilized for other useful purposes.

3-4 WHAT IS "SET IN ORDER"?

"Set in Order" is to determine how to place items at specific locations with clear visual information in order to allow the effortless retrieval of necessary items. Every item must be given a specific location for storage and handled by following predetermined rules. Then items must be clearly labeled with visual information in order to allow easy identification of items by any worker. In short, the implementation level of "Set in Order" in a workplace signifies how well different items are managed around us.

ALLOWING EFFORTLESS RETRIEVAL OF NECESSARY ITEMS

All items must be stored in a specific way, at all times, so that they can be obtained immediately when necessary without searching at all. What I mean by "immediately" is within approximately 30 seconds. To maintain this it is equally important for every employee to always return items to the specific locations they were retrieved from.

3 FACTORS OF "SET IN ORDER"

"Set in Order" involves the following important components to consider: placement location, placing, and visual indication. It is important to identify the significance of these factors and take them into consideration when implementing the principle of "Set in Order" in a thorough manner. Otherwise, workers will fail to return items to their proper designated locations and will become more confused as to where to retrieve necessary items. The most effective method of ensuring that these 3 factors are always followed is to make these components into a must-follow checklist and standardize the whole process of storing and retrieving items across the organization.

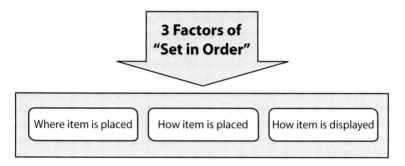

3 Factors of "Set in Order"

| Where item is placed | How item is placed | How item is displayed |

Allows items to be returned to their designated locations easily

Figure 3.3 Factors of "Set in Order"

3-5 WHAT IS "SHINE"?

MEANING OF "SHINE"

"Shine" is creating a clean and trash-free work environment by continuous cleaning practices. Many people think that "Shine" simply means cleaning the workplace for the sole purpose of making it spotless. I understand that being spotless is important for hospitals, however it is more important to understand the constructive meaning and implications behind "Shine." "Shine" really means to manage items you use often carefully in order to maintain top working conditions at all times, by following a certain set of rules. It is also equally important to separate clean items from dirty items and clean, in fine detail, all workplaces in order to prevent in-hospital infections from occurring.

PERFORM INSPECTION WHILE CLEANING

"Shine" is mainly for working toward attaining cleanliness, however it also involves performing inspection while you are Shining. Inspections while cleaning should monitor checkpoints, such as determining whether or not every part of a workplace is in sanitary condition, items are put back in their original locations as rules dictate, and visual information, including name labels, are intact. For example, when a piece of medical equipment is found to be malfunctioning, such routine inspections allow a worker to immediately report the fault and submit a request for an appropriate mitigation measure.

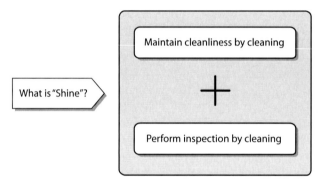

Figure 3.4 "Shine" is Essentially Inspection

3-6 WHAT IS "STANDARDIZE"?

MEANING OF "STANDARDIZE"

"Standardize" ensures that "Sort," "Set in Order," and "Shine" are consistently carried out and a clean environment is constantly maintained. A key point to consider when performing "Standardize" is how we can effectively manage our workplace to ensure that it is always kept as clean as desired. What is required to manage the 3S's ("Sort," "Set in Order," and "Shine") is setting up rules and standardizing operating procedures. By the same token, the establishment of Visual Management systems is also essential to making sure that a working team always follows such rules and standardized work.

WHAT IS VISUAL MANAGEMENT?

Visual Management is the ability to easily detect, by sight, abnormalities within an environment so that appropriate actions can be immediately taken. This purpose alone ought to be one of the main reasons for implementing Clinical 5S in hospitals. For instance, when an I.V. stand or wheel chair is placed outside the bounds of where they need to be stored, workers should be able to realize this abnormality by simply looking at the situation alone. Visual Management creates a hospital workplace where issues and abnormalities can be easily detected by the consistent utilization of Clinical 5S. In other words, it can be said that the cleanliness of a workplace is maintained as long as the establishment of Visual Management is solidly in place.

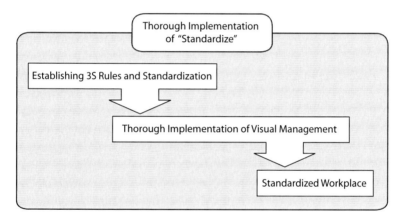

Figure 3.5 Creating a Standardized Workplace

3-7 WHAT IS "SUSTAIN"?

MEANING OF "SUSTAIN"

"Sustain" means to develop a habit through discipline, with which rules are always respected and carried out in any situation. The important point here is "to develop a habit through discipline," which requires a dedication in every single person to follow the same set of rules repeatedly. If one carries out the same action over and over, they would feel restless if they did not perform it as usual. They could even reach a point where they completed performing the task without even realizing it. This level of competency can be communicated as "developing a habit through discipline."

THE PURPOSE OF AN ACTION MUST BE UNDERSTOOD BEFORE DEVELOPING A HABIT THROUGH DISCIPLINE

What is important in becoming accustomed to performing a certain task in predetermined way? I mentioned before that the repetitiveness of performing a certain action is necessary. However, technically speaking, the ability to maintain the discipline of repeating the same bodily movement is more critical. In order to nourish such a discipline, workers must fully acknowledge the meaning and justification behind the action they are about to internalize.

While watching a baseball game on TV, a commentator, who was also an active baseball coach, caught my attention by making an interesting remark about his coaching experiences. He said:

"Back when I was a baseball player, I, along with other team members, simply followed what the coach instructed us to do — such as how we ought to practice together. This is because there was a huge gap between the coach and us in terms of status and our understanding of the game itself. However, in recent years I feel that this gap has shrunken as young players become much more knowledgeable about baseball. For this reason young players may still look like they are listening to what the coach is saying but if they are not persuaded, or if they disagree with the coach, they are simply reluctant to continue playing as instructed. Therefore coaches are making extra effort to persuade players by having discussions so that both sides can agree upon a certain way of practicing."

What we can learn from this insight is that continuity cannot be sustained without persuasion. Younger generations, especially, have a strong tendency to refuse to act as told when they disagree. A strong will is absolutely essential to ensure continuity in one's behavior. As well, a person must acknowledge the true meaning and justification behind each action. I believe that this is the very source of one's willingness to continue performing predetermined tasks.

CHAPTER 4

PRACTICAL GUIDELINES FOR IMPLEMENTING CLINICAL 5S

4-1 IMPLEMENTATION GUIDELINES FOR CLINICAL 5S

IN THIS CHAPTER, I WILL describe the overview of procedures in implementing Clinical 5S.

BASIC STEP 1: FORMULATE A PLAN OF ACTION FOR CLINICAL 5S IMPLEMENTATION

The main requirements of this first step are to establish a system for adapting Clinical 5S activities, to clearly identify the objectives of Clinical 5S, and to conduct strategy planning for overall Clinical 5S implementation tactics across the entire hospital. The most important step is to designate an implementation committee within the hospital, as well as designating a committed chairperson of the committee.

Basic Step 2: Conduct Clinical 5S implementation Workshop Training

Frankly speaking, there is almost no difficult technique or logic involved in practicing the necessary duties of Clinical 5S. We need to remember that the important point is whether or not enough time can be allocated to carry out Clinical 5S activities on a regular basis. There are many cases where necessary 5S activities do not get carried out, whatever the excuse may be. To avoid this, it is extremely important to make sure that the true intention and value of implementing Clinical 5S in the workplace is clearly acknowledged and appreciated by every staff member in the hospital. This leads to the importance of education, which can be done through various training workshops. I believe that experts outside your hospital should do the training, as workers tend to follow the instructions of outside experts much more willingly than those that come from within.

Basic Step 3: Execute "Sort"

"Sort" should begin by taking an objective action, such as throwing away unnecessary items from the workplace in a thorough manner. However, there are many items found unnecessary in the hospital which we often feel reluctant to get rid of. It is important that we make strong decisions to dispose of unnecessary items at all times, as a successful implementation of Clinical 5S heavily depends upon whether or not we are able to execute "Sort" correctly and in a comprehensive manner.

Basic Step 4: Execute "Set in Order"

"Set in Order" is the most time-consuming activity. In the process of executing "Set in Order" you will begin to experience the positive effects of Clinical 5S. "Set in Order" clearly defines how each item should be stored in its designated location, which is accompanied by a solid set of rules as to how visual indications should be presented throughout the hospital. Most importantly, how "Set in Order" ought to be executed must be standardized among the different departments in order to promise a thorough implementation of the "Set in Order" principle.

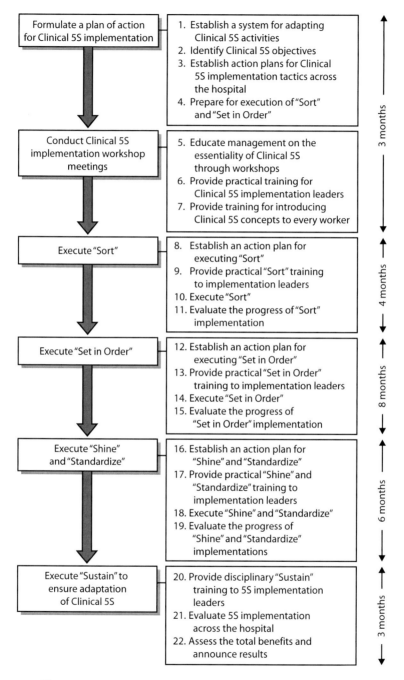

Figure 4.1 Practical Guidelines for Implementing Clinical 5S

Basic Step 5: Execute "Shine" and "Standardize"

A set of standards for cleaning has to be established prior to initiating "Shine." Such standards should clearly identify instructions for cleaning every inch of the hospital, with the full participation of the staff, and should be shared among different departments. The main purpose of "Standardize" is to construct the foundation for a Visual Management system so that "Sort," "Set in Order," and "Shine" can be performed at all times.

Basic Step 6: Execute "Sustain" to ensure adaptation of Clinical 5S

The most important aspect of Clinical 5S is to fully enforce a thorough use of "Sustain." In fact, many hospitals have incorporated Clinical 5S initially for the purpose of introducing a degree of discipline into the organization. In order to implement "Sustain" in a thorough manner, every staff member must be persuaded that Clinical 5S is absolutely essential to ensuring efficient operations within the organization. However, ensuring "Sustain" is another time-consuming step.

4-2 Formulating a Plan of Action for Clinical 5S Implementation

In implementing Clinical 5S, we need to establish an all-inclusive system for 5S to identify objectives and carry out careful strategy planning in order to promote 5S activities. Establishing a Clinical 5S expediting mechanism is especially critical for ensuring positive results in the long run. It should not be simply one or two departments carrying out Clinical 5S; the whole organization must devote itself to adapting Clinical 5S collectively. I am sure that this mentality also applies to many activities within hospitals other than 5S.

On the other hand, the hospital as a whole often fails to become motivated to directing its collective effort toward Clinical 5S, since performing regular 5S activities are considered a relatively common sense type of work. To avoid this, an all-inclusive system for Clinical 5S is absolutely necessary to promote systematic and organizational strategies in Clinical 5S adaptation across the organization.

There are 3 fundamental philosophies for implementing Clinical 5S in a systematic manner:

1. Creating the right mindset
2. Establishing the right mechanism
3. Managing execution

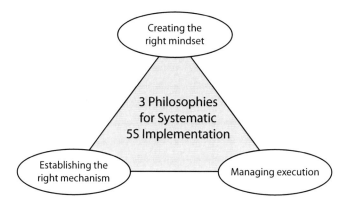

Figure 4.2 Fundamental Philosophies for Implementing Clinical 5S

4-3 CREATING THE RIGHT MINDSET

What is basically meant by "creating the right mindset" is how we can draw out motivation in every worker to practice Clinical 5S diligently. Whether or not Clinical 5S can be successfully implemented depends on the spirit of commitment among workers. Therefore the mindset of the management team and implementation leaders is extremely important; so workers can simulate the same type of positive attitudes. Doctors, department directors, and section leaders who are usually in the position of making important decisions must take the initiative to possess the right mindset themselves.

In addition, a positive atmosphere that allows for the effective adaptation of Clinical 5S across the entire organization must be set in place. Of course, such a desired atmosphere has a prerequisite of having every worker engaged, with positive attitudes, toward battling the challenges of Clinical 5S implementation. Some of the effective strategies for creating a positive mindset across the organization are to create awareness posters, Clinical 5S badges, and accept suggestions for Clinical 5S slogans from active workers. Touring of "5S-ed" manufacturing facilities or other successful hospitals can also provide workers with strong inspiration and many useful ideas as to what the hospital can look like in the future.

Training Supervisors and Managers

Kick-off Meeting

Factory and Hospital Tours

Collect 5S Ideas from Workers

Creating the Right Mindset Toward 5S Activities

5S Awareness Posters

Collect 5S Slogans from Workers

Visiting other Departments and Workplaces

Training Implementation Leaders

Figure 4.3 Creating the Right Mindset

These activities are often utilized for the purpose of turning normally passive-minded workers into active participants in a new project. It is important to acknowledge that overcoming the challenge of adapting Clinical 5S with the full participation of workers creates many other opportunities for achieving other continuous improvement results as well.

Figure 4.4 describes some examples of slogans that can be used. Additionally, any activities that bring a sense of enlightenment to the workplace, such as Clinical 5S, require all workers to share the same values and objectives, for which the top executives must proactively fulfill the leading roles in promoting and managing.

"5S is the foundation of eradicating medical malpractices."

"Create a hospital that patients can fully trust by implementing 5S."

"Change organizational culture by 5S."

"Eliminate Waste (Muda), Irrationality (Muri), Inconsistency (Mura) by 5S."

"Eliminate the occurrence of errors on Gemba."

"Create a workplace that can be easily visualized."

"Maintain a Shiny (Pika Pika) workplace."

"Start by comprehensive cleaning with everyone's full participation."

"Zero work errors through 5S implementation."

Figure 4.4 Examples of Clinical 5S Slogans

4-4 ESTABLISHING THE RIGHT MECHANISM

A well-designed operational mechanism needs to be established in order to keep Clinical 5S activities running smoothly. Such a mechanism should promote the effective sharing of critical information in regard to the progress of Clinical 5S implementation and continue to generate positive energy for driving Clinical 5S activities forward. Such an effective mechanism for promoting Clinical 5S also needs to be customized according to the varying needs of hospitals. In many cases the mechanism must be kept simple. Generally speaking, hospitals have designated promotion committees or project teams for initiating new activities. It is a good idea to make use of such groups to seek assistance on designing the most appropriate mechanism.

DESIGNING AN IMPLEMENTATION COMMITTEE

When expanding Clinical 5S activities, practical guidelines for objective activities, such as "Sort" and "Set in Order," need to be formulated. However, more importantly, we need to make sure that such activities get carried out throughout the organization at a desired frequency. It cannot be said that Clinical 5S is implemented truthfully if the level of Clinical 5S competency improves only in a certain department within the hospital. In order to promote Clinical 5S effectively across the organization, a defragmented implementation committee must be put together to oversee the entire implementation process. There are many types of implementation committees, according to the size and distinct characteristics of each hospital. I will give here the basic description of what an effective implementation committee looks like and present you with explanations for the roles of each organizational segment.

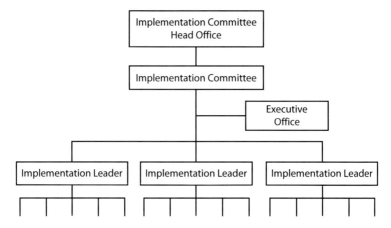

Figure 4.5 Example of Clinical 5S Organizational Structure

IMPLEMENTATION COMMITTEE HEAD OFFICE

The head office establishes implementation policies and sets the overall direction for the whole organization to follow, in terms of Clinical 5S implementation. The head office also approves suggestions submitted from the implementation committee based upon the decisions of the top executive, which is usually the hospital head.

IMPLEMENTATION COMMITTEE

The committee submits various suggestions related to improving the level of Clinical 5S implementation and is the central role for yielding and managing organizational progress. In most cases, department or section leaders are given the responsibility of running such a committee.

IMPLEMENTATION EXECUTIVE OFFICE

The executive office performs many responsibilities, such as the designing of training curriculums, promotion and preparation of Clinical 5S activities, and moderating meetings held by the implementation committee.

IMPLEMENTATION LEADER

The implementation leader is solely responsible for putting Clinical 5S into action. In many cases, existing manager-class personnel, such as the supervisor of a workplace or leaders of smaller project groups, are assigned to perform this duty.

The most important responsibilities of these organizational structures is to suggest new ideas and methodologies, as well as execute these new suggestions in a practical manner, in order to maintain the vitality of Clinical 5S activities. Traditionally speaking, what we call "organizations" or "systems" tend to easily become fragmented and discouraged after time, which could eventually cause Clinical 5S activities to be viewed as unworthy of their continuous effort, not to mention positive results could no longer be derived from 5S. In order to prevent this we need to make sure to include in the committee someone who is obsessed with practicing 5S and is passionate enough that they will never give up; that will continue to preach the absolute necessity and virtue of Clinical 5S to other departments or colleagues.

ESTABLISHING THE GROUND WORK (INFRASTRUCTURE) FOR IMPLEMENTING CLINICAL 5S

Certain conditions and environments have to be met in order to ensure an effective implementation of Clinical 5S.

A. SECURE STORAGE SPACE IN A WAREHOUSE

First, a sufficient amount of storage space must be allocated so that "Sort" can be carried out effectively. In many cases you run into situations where unnecessary items cannot be thrown away immediately; especially items such as large medical devices, or supplies that are kept unused for a long period of time. If such items continue to be left alone, even with Red Tags attached to them, they would keep hindering the implementation of Clinical 5S to a significant degree. That is the reason why sufficient space must be allocated across the hospital for temporarily storing unnecessary items that cannot immediately be disposed of.

B. Design a purchasing plan for supplies needed

As implementation takes place, various departments will ask you to purchase essential supplies such as desks, file cabinets, file folders, etc. Therefore it is important to establish fundamental guidelines in advance of how to effectively respond to such demands from 5S practitioners. However, most importantly, we must make an effort to avoid purchasing additional items right away. If new storage shelves or spaces are needed, we first need to examine the situation and try our best to create additional storage shelf space with existing materials by applying our creativity.

C. Establish a budget for implementation

Of course, there is a limitation to our creativity and we sometimes have to purchase new supplies. The important thing is not to start buying supplies in a random manner or you will end up with more waste. A careful budget plan must be carried out and purchasing activities should follow the budgetary requirements at all times.

D. Designate dedicated time for performing Clinical 5S activities

One of the reasons why Clinical 5S fails to progress forward is the lack of time allocated for carrying out specific 5S activities. I understand that some hospitals are truly suffering from overwhelming time schedules or time conflicts, however in many organizations the lack of time is often used as an excuse for their inability to maintain Clinical 5S activities. In order to avoid such an excuse it is important to formally designate an appropriate amount of time to administer 5S. As a guide approximately one hour per week should be allocated, which may need to be adjusted as this may be insufficient in some cases. The key here is establishing a strategic time allocation plan according to a specific implementation plan and timeline, as determined by the hospital.

Prepare implementation action plans

Formulating strategic planning manuals is crucial to implementing Clinical 5S. Based upon such manuals, an appropriate course of action has to be chosen and managed. I will describe the ways to manage the execution of these actions in later chapters, however here I will explain how to lay out strategic planning.

Basically speaking, strategic planning manuals for Clinical 5S are created in order to identify unique action plans to effectively carry out "Sort," "Set in Order," and "Shine" for different areas of the hospital. It is recommended that these manuals be created by implementation leaders and approved by their managers. Appropriate templates, as well as the format of such planning manuals, should be freely discussed in implementation committee meetings. The following are necessary discussion points to be included in planning manuals:

- Applicable areas for "Sort," "Set in Order," and "Shine" activities
- The person in charge for each applicable area
- Scheduling
- Photographs of applicable areas (before implementation)
- Physically attach "Set in Order" instructions/ checklist(s) to applicable areas

Even though these planning manuals are utilized as implementation management tools, the most important aspect is the process of determining what the manuals should include and creating them according to those rules. The true value in this process is to yield a higher level of motivation toward practicing Clinical 5S by allowing each member of the implementation group to proactively exchange unique opinions as to what planning manuals should look like and how they should function. Then managers should use their expertise to decide whether or not to approve such planning manuals before they are put into practice.

CREATE A MECHANISM TO ALLOW SHARING OF CLINICAL 5S IMPLEMENTATION KNOW-HOW

As the implementation of Clinical 5S progresses, each workplace will begin to have its own unique implementation know-how and strategy. Sharing such information among workplaces is crucial as new know-how can act as a stimulus to other teams conducting their 5S activities. In order to promote the sharing of such critical information, the following methods are proven to be effective:

Idea suggestion sheet for Clinical 5S

This is for submitting continuous improvement ideas and case studies that are related to Clinical 5S. Existing continuous improvement suggestion sheets can also be used if you already have them in place.

Clinical 5S public information board

This information board should display submitted Clinical 5S continuous improvement suggestions and be made available so that everyone can learn the information.

Utilize internet or intranet for information sharing

If an information network system, such as an intranet, has already been established in the hospital, the information about improvement ides and case studies can be effectively shared by posting it on dedicated websites or online bulletins. I know that it will put a little bit of burden on the bandwidth in some hospitals but attaching digital photographs to the messages will make the information more valuable.

Visit other workplaces to learn progress

Touring each other's workplace promotes much more meaningful sharing of continuous improvement know-how. Tension will rise for those workers who are being welcomed by their colleagues from another workplace for a tour and, for that, they will be inspired to work harder at achieving Clinical 5S benefits in their own workplace.

Through creating these various opportunities for information to be shared, as described above, the level of Clinical 5S competency across the hospital will improve drastically in an enlivened manner.

4-5 MANAGEMENT OF ACTION PLANS

MANAGING THE PROGRESS OF ACTION PLANS

The implementation status of Clinical 5S activities has to be assessed based upon specified plans of action. Generally speaking, implementation-planning reports often fail to be evaluated after submission. That is why responsible Clinical 5S supervisors, such as department or section leaders, are required to manage progress, including the evaluation of various progress reports.

The main purpose of Clinical 5S progress management is to evaluate whether or not necessary activities have been implemented according to the submitted plans of action, as well as to provide specific practical and technical instructions in order to yield the desired results. In this step we need to focus on how to introduce and administer implementation rather than analyzing the overall quality of Clinical 5S that is being adapted. I will describe here some important key elements in assessing the implementation progress of Clinical 5S.

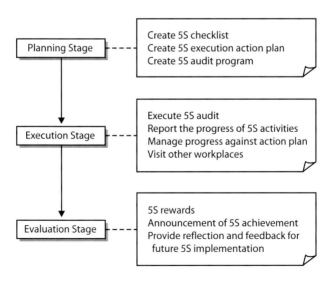

Figure 4.6 Flow of Implementation/Execution Management

MAKE VISIBLE THE GAP BETWEEN A PLAN OF ACTION AND WHAT IS BEING DONE

As we all know, things do not always go as planned. Therefore it is important to acknowledge what is in conflict with the plan of action, which should be mutually understood by both managers and implementation leaders, by comparing the actual progress against what is expected. This is especially important when there is a delay in the implementation process; in other words, expected results are not being acquired in a timely manner. The true cause of the delay must be identified and carefully scrutinized.

If such a delay is discovered to be due to the negligence of implementors or inherent ineffectiveness within the plan of action itself, a strict reinforcement of proper guidance must be provided to responsible leaders of the implementation groups. On the other hand, you may run into situations where everything is beyond your control, such as when the hospital hinders or terminates your plans at its own convenience. In such a case managers must work diligently toward removing such organizational obstacles by conducting a series of hearings in order to understand the real challenges that workers are facing in implementing Clinical 5S in their workplaces.

DETERMINE THAT THE PROPER ACTIONS, WHICH REQUIRE FULL PARTICIPATION FROM THE TEAM, ARE CHOSEN

One of the prerequisites for a successful Clinical 5S implementation is the full participation of team members. In many cases that I have observed, only the implementation leader is carrying out activities in a proactive manner instead of performing supervisory responsibilities over his team members, who often maintain a passive compliance. This can be quite problematic from the perspective of an effective Clinical 5S adaptation. It is given that implementation leaders are expected to guide their team members through the process with strong leadership skills, however, more importantly, leaders must allocate responsibilities among the team members and ensure that they actively carry out the necessary implementation actions in a consistent manner.

4-6 OVERVIEW OF CLINICAL 5S IMPLEMENTATION TRAINING

EDUCATION FOR MANAGERS

It is safe to say that a successful Clinical 5S implementation is entirely in the hands of managers. Hospitals will never succeed without an appreciation and understanding of the true benefits of Clinical 5S from its managers. For instance, if the desks of managers are always messy, their basic attitudes must be immediately changed and should be done so voluntarily.

Let us think about what is important in educating managers. The most significant aspect is to have managers realize their own lack of appreciation for 5S and to raise their level of urgency for adapting 5S into their own work environment. One effective method to raise manager's awareness of the issue is to present them with photographs of their existing workplace conditions. Studying the photos, on which problem areas can be pointed out, is much more effective than observing workplaces with the naked eye and also enables such managers to acknowledge the lack of their dedication. More importantly, managers must realize that it is their negative attitude toward 5S that creates an undesirable atmosphere for workers to be in to promote an effective implementation of Clinical 5S.

MANAGEMENT SKILLS DETERMINE THE QUALITY OF CLINICAL 5S

The fact that "the final quality of Clinical 5S implementation represents the level of management strength within a hospital" must be clearly understood. Generally speaking, managers who do not recognize the significance of Clinical 5S underestimate how Clinical 5S can transform the hospital as a whole. Such mangers tend to have strong beliefs, such as "Safety has nothing to do with Clinical 5S," "Clinical 5S does not remove wastes," or "Good services are not directly related to Clinical 5S." Moreover, they frequently fail to have an essential attitude that could have allowed them to cherish the fundamental elements of work itself. If managers do not change it will be extremely challenging to maintain medical safety and ensure patients the level of comfort that they deserve.

CARRY OUT MANAGEMENT TRAINING BASED ON PRACTICALITY

As I described before, managers must understand that the final outcome of Clinical 5S implementation depends heavily upon their management skills, therefore it is important to develop training programs that concentrate upon improving management skills. However, such management training often puts emphasis merely on various theories and fails to cover their practicality, so management training in Clinical 5S has to be carried out in strong accordance with how management philosophies can be put to real use in order to acquire true results. I cannot stress enough that certain sets of agreed upon rules must be followed at all times to effectively continue Clinical 5S, and for that a relatively high level of management skill is absolutely essential. I will describe in Figure 4.7 (on page 46) examples of management training.

EDUCATION FOR SUPERVISORS AND CLINICAL 5S IMPLEMENTATION LEADERS

Specific training content has to be established for supervisors and Clinical 5S implementation leaders. The absolute necessity of Clinical 5S and awareness of urgency for Clinical 5S, as well as practical guidance for adapting 5S, must be taught first. Please refer to Figure 4.7 for examples of training to cover these principles.

At this level of training the teaching of specific Clinical 5S implementation procedures is emphasized. This type of training is extremely valuable as it gets other general staff involved, which in the long run creates an image of how Clinical 5S ought to be adapted throughout the organization.

FOCUS ON ESTABLISHING A COLLECTIVE VISION OF "SET IN ORDER" AND ITS PRACTICAL ADAPTATION TECHNIQUES

I will describe here a specific form of training through which workers can learn how to effectively implement the concept of "Standardize" in their workplaces. The most important purpose of this training is to enable staff members to become capable of clearly identifying a certain level at which their practice of "Standardize" can be considered to have reached acceptably competent. In other words, it is important for workers to share this type of a collective vision toward how "Standardize" should be adapted within the hospital environment.

Practical methodologies and know-how for adapting "Standardize" also have to be shared among the staff. When you share such information freely, implementation members from different teams will meet with each other to discuss every single problematic area in their workplaces and analyze how applying "Standardize" principles can eliminate the issues. Then, participants create sketches that include collective visions and timelines for meeting the requirements of "Standardize," as well as useful key points or secrets to ensure continuous results.

INTEGRATE ON-THE-JOB TRAINING

After having analyzed a few workplaces to identify problems and provide strategies, workers will begin to understand the meaning of administering the "Standardize" principle and become capable of knowing at what point an implementation of "Standardize" is considered satisfactory by their organization. This type of training should be conducted on the job as much as possible. Training where both supervisors and 5S leaders, who are the trainees in this case, are required to identify issues in workplaces and formulate continuous improvement strategies on their own, as well as creating a sketch to visually summarize their solutions and plan of action, is extremely important. Such a sketch is later put into practice, which is proven to be an effective method for ensuring positive results.

Workshop Schedule for 5S Managers

Target Trainee: Section Managers
Duration: 2 days

◆ **Goals:**

> 1. To understand the importance and true meaning of 5S as well as fundamental management principles for implementing Clinical 5S
> 2. To analyze various hindrances to Clinical 5S implementation through understanding the innate characteristics of Clinical 5S

	Day 1	Day 2
9:00 ... 12:00	1. Orientation - Objectives and action plans 2. Roles of Managers - Functions and roles of managers - What is management?	Debrief on study topics from Day 1 7. Discuss systemized Clinical 5S implementation measures - Designate Clinical 5S Implementation Committee - Define targeted subjects and areas for Clinical 5S implementation - Establish Clinical 5S objectives
	Lunch	Lunch
13:00 ... 18:00	3. Importance of Clinical 5S - Clinical 5S and human error - Clinical 5S and prevention of medical malpractices - Clinical 5S and operational wastes 4. What is clinical 5S? - Meaning of "Sort" and "Set in Order" - Meaning of "Shine," "Standardize," and "Sustain" 5. Understand the present situation of Clinical 5S - Analyze real world examples of Clinical 5S	Small group discussions 8. Action plan for "Sort" and "Set in Order" - Formulate standards for "Sort" - Formulate common rules for "Set in Order" - Discuss practical action plans for implementing "Sort" and "Set in Order" Presentation and feedback
	Dinner	
19:00 ... 21:00	6. Analysis of hindrances to Clinical 5S implementation Group Discussion	

Figure 4.7 Example Workshop Schedule for 5S Managers

4-7 SETTING GOALS FOR CLINICAL 5S ACTIVITIES AND IMPLEMENTATION PLANNING

WHAT IS GOAL SETTING?

The setting of goals mentioned here signifies the establishment of a desired competency level and measures ought to be taken in order to reach that level. Managing Clinical 5S activities starts with setting clear objectives. Such objectives are designed for the organization as a whole, which calls for a collective effort in order to allow a successful implementation of Clinical 5S in the long run. An important aspect in this process is whether or not the members of the organization can show full consent to the set objectives, in terms of the organization's ideal level of competency and directions. Such objectives should not be obtrusive or compromising.

When implementing Clinical 5S it is extremely important to convince workers of the reasons why Clinical 5S needs to be adapted on an organizational level and is absolutely necessary in every single workplace throughout the hospital. Each staff member must not only understand the necessity but also go as far as internalizing the challenge and have a sense of urgency toward implementation.

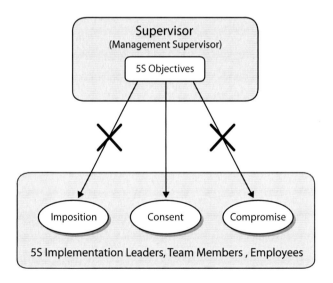

Figure 4.8 Importance of Acquiring Consent

SETTING GOALS FOR PRACTICING CLINICAL 5S

What are the key elements that have to be included in goals set for implementing Clinical 5S? Such goals have to specifically designate the following aspects: "What?" as in specific objectives, "To what degree?" as in competency level, and "By when?" as in timeline. I will describe some examples below.

EXAMPLES OF SETTING GOALS

Goal #1: To establish the foundation for preventing medical malpractices.

Item	Content
Objective	Establishing the foundation for preventing medical malpractices
Competency Level	50% decrease in the number of human errors
Timeline (Duration)	1 year

Table 4.1 Goal Setting, Goal #1

Goal #2: To transform organizational culture into a desirable one.

Item	Content
Objective	Transforming organizational culture
Competency Level	To the point where staff can proactively seek and attain continuous improvement by themselves
Timeline (Duration)	1 year

Table 4.2 Goal Setting, Goal #2

Formulating action plans for Clinical 5S

The process of planning appropriate actions is absolutely indispensable for reaching the objectives of any given task in an effective manner. Activities without careful planning can never lead to solid results. Action planning for Clinical 5S can be divided into "Integral Planning" and "Individual Planning," which is also known as Clinical 5S Execution Planning. Integral Planning proposes activities to be carried out by the whole organization. On the other hand, Individual Planning designs specific actions uniquely for "Sort," "Set in Order," and "Shine" for each specific area to follow. Refer to Figure 4.9 for content to be discussed under both categories of planning.

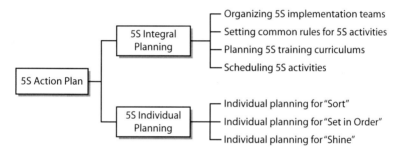

Figure 4.9 Overview of Clinical 5S Action Plan

Formulating a Clinical 5S integral planning manual

Clinical 5S's Integral Planning involves scheduling many important organizational functions, such as installing responsible teams for ensuring 5S activities will continue, establishing common objective and rules, and conducting training and workshops to spread the knowledge of Clinical 5S.

Refer to Figure 4.10 for an example of what Integral Planning may look like in practice. As shown in the figure, it generally requires 3 years for hospitals to reach their desired competency level of "Sort," "Set in Order," and "Shine" activity standards, as specified by their unique objectives.

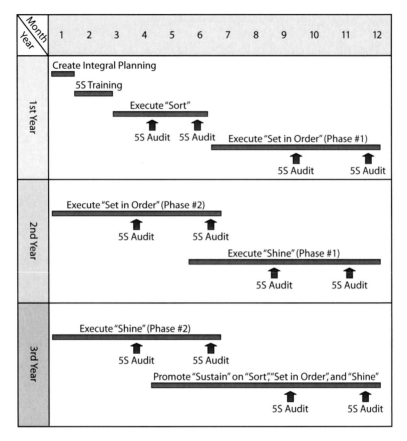

Figure 4.10 Clinical 5S Integral Planning Schedule

FORMULATING CLINICAL 5S INDIVIDUAL PLANNING MANUALS

Clinical 5S Individual Planning has to be done in detail and separately for each of the 3S activities ("Sort," "Set in Order," and "Shine"). For each 3S activity, a careful planning of appropriate actions, including key players and activity content, has to be performed and summarized into a form of instructions.

"Sort", "Set in Order", "Shine" Action Plan		Affiliation	Creator	Date of Creation
Target Area	Administered by	Plan		Score

Affiliation............... Department you belong to

Creator................... Clinical 5S Leader is listed here

Date of Creation...... Indicate when the action plan is announced

Target Area............. List areas where "Sort", "Set in Order", and "Shine" will be applied
(Examples)
- Nurse station work tables
- Medical supply storage/shelves
- Reception counter

Administrator .... Name of the person or team that carries out actions

Plan...................... Execution schedules

Score .... Managers evaluate results according to objectives
A - Progress according to schedule
B - Some delay / behind schedule
C - No progress according to action plan

Figure 4.11 Clinical 5S Individual Action Plan

4-8 Key Points to Remember when Implementing Clinical 5S

Key Point #1

Do not force doctors to participate at an early stage of implementation.

> Generally speaking, technicians show little interest in adopting 5S in a factory setting, and it is likely doctors are the same way in hospitals. If we force doctors to participate in 5S activities they will immediately show their disagreement with and rejection of 5S. Therefore, it is important for us to take an approach in which doctors do not feel forced to attend 5S practices at an early stage of implementation. However, we need to make sure that doctors are also then asked to not interfere with or discourage any implementation activities for the time being.

KEY POINT #2

It is important to eventually have doctors participate.
> A recommendation that doctors should not be forced to participate at all does not comply with the fundamental philosophy behind 5S. Many nurses sincerely request that doctors, exclusively, are the people that should play the leadership roles in adapting 5S. On the other hand, it is somewhat justifiable to exempt doctors from participating, given the current hospital organizational structures and difficult positions that doctors often find themselves in. However, we must continue to seek the involvement of doctors by not only teaching them 5S logic and theories, but also persuading them of the absolute necessity and true values of implementing 5S through presenting positive results acquired by actual practices.

KEY POINT #3

Save time by removing wasteful operations and use that time to care for patients in better ways. Having a notion that the prevention of medical accidents can be achieved in this process is important.
> As you all know, hospitals are categorized as being in the service industry. The true value of hospital operations is to provide patients with the highest level of service and satisfaction. This sounds pretty obvious, however, many organizations, regardless of the industry they are in, often fail to achieve what is simply considered to be common sense. The fact that hospitals can become capable of eliminating malpractices through implementing Clinical 5S provides the highest level of added value to patients. To achieve this our energy should be guided toward ensuring safe and satisfying medical services to patients through eliminating wasted time and resources by adapting Clinical 5S in a comprehensive manner.

KEY POINT #4

Promote standardization of various operations.
> As Clinical 5S is implemented, you will begin to see a level of inconsistency for a given operation across different departments. It is important to reduce this inconsistency

as much as possible by standardizing operations. For example, nurse stations located in each hospital ward may have different workplace layouts and different ways of labeling medicines, as well as using different furnishing supplies to divide patient rooms. Standardization of operations through Clinical 5S is an effective method for eliminating such differences among departments. This is especially important when a shift change occurs in a nurse station; not only nurses but also other staff members will be able to prevent errors and perform transitional duties without difficulties, as long as standardization of their operations is achieved at all times.

Key Point #5

Do not prepare a budget from the get-go.

Any Clinical 5S implementation requires a certain amount of budget. For examples, purchasing additional storage shelves, cans of paint, and label makers will be necessary at some point. However, if we need additional storage shelves or cases, the first thing we must attempt is to make better use of the existing storage spaces by applying "Sort" activities. This is the type of mindset everyone has to accommodate. If everyone can entertain this approach our very first proposition will not be asking for an allocation of a budget. We also need to maintain a positive attitude, in which it is only when we have used up our ideas and creativity that we can start considering establishing a budget, if necessary.

Key Point #6

Know how to deal with excuses.

You will receive many different excuses from workplaces that have not been successful in adapting 5S activities. It is important to apply your management skills to dealing with excuses in an effective manner so that your staff will stop trying to justify their incompetence at adaptation with selfish reasons. I cannot stress enough that a successful implementation of Clinical 5S heavily depends upon the level of management in your organization.

CHAPTER 5

HOW TO IMPLEMENT "SORT"

5-1 IMPLEMENTATION PROCEDURES FOR "SORT"

THE BASIC STEPS IN ADAPTING "Sort" are described below and must be put into action along with an appropriate timeline.

- Carry out preliminary preparations prior to "Sort" execution
- The person in charge makes a judgment if an item is necessary or not
- Consolidate unnecessary items in one place
- Managers decide if an item is necessary or not
- Tag unnecessary items (Red Tagging)
- Immediate disposal of unnecessary items
- Dispose of unnecessary (Red Tagged) items after a fixed period of non-use

ITEMS TO COVER DURING A PRELIMINARY PREPARATION PRIOR
TO "SORT"

Performing an essential preliminary preparation is crucial
to carrying out "Sort" in an efficient and timely manner.

1. Setting standards for "Sort."

   Setting standards allows us to draw a clear line in order
   to identify whether items are necessary or unnecessary.
   Such standards also create a certain set of rules to be followed, up until the disposal of the unnecessary items.

2. Maintain designated holding areas for unnecessary items.

   Items identified to be unnecessary are collectively stored
   in one place and are later thrown away by a disposal service provider. For the time being, specific areas need to be
   designated for temporarily storing unnecessary items.

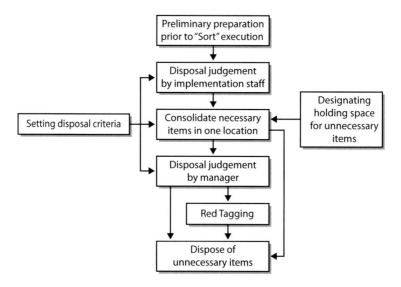

Figure 5.1 Implementation Procedures for "Sort"

3. Prepare Red Tags.

   Red Tags are used for items where it cannot be immediately determined whether they are necessary or not.
   Tagged items are stored for a fixed duration. The tags
   will enable us to officially identify such items as completely unnecessary if they were not used at all during
   the holding time.

4. Prepare plan of action documents to implement "Sort."

Action plans to implement "Sort" need to be prepared and documented here. As for formulating such documents, please refer to Figures 4.9 thru 4.11 on pages 49-51.

5-2 Setting Standards for "Sort"

What are standards for "Sort"?

Setting standards and rules allow us to practice "Sort" smoothly. Standards for "Sort" include criteria for which items can be identified as unnecessary, as well as provide us with useful guidelines and procedures to reach the point of making that judgment. Some laws and regulations may not allow us to hold certain items. We may also have difficulties in disposing of items that have amortized values. In these cases, it is important to make clear what type of procedures and applications are required to accommodate these restricted items.

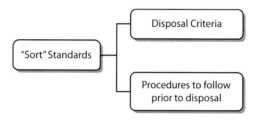

Figure 5.2 "Sort" Standards

What is the "Disposal Criteria"

"Sort" is essentially the art of disposing of items. The secret is to have the courage to throw away, once and for all, any items that you determine to be unnecessary. However, when you make your own decision to do so, your supervisors or colleagues may criticize you for your action because they may believe that items can still serve a useful purpose in the future. This is primarily why your workplace remains cluttered with useless items and documents. In order to administer "Sort" in a timely fashion, official formulas for standardizing the process of the decision of whether to throw certain items away or not is absolutely necessary. The basic rule is that such formulae should be established by each hospital or workplace, based upon its special requirements.

Item	Description
Documents	- Dispose of documents that have not been used for at least 1 year - Dispose of documents that have exceeded their shelf life - If documents are stored in great quantity, keep only one copy and throw away the rest - Dispose of copied documents and keep only the originals
Fixtures and Furniture	- Dispose of broken or unusable items - Dispose of items that have not been used for over 2 years - Store items that are not currently used separately
Medical Supplies	- Do not store more than a 3 day supply of items in any workplace - Do not store more than a 1 week supply of items in stocking warehouses - Dispose of medical supplies that can no longer be used
Medicines	- Dispose of medicines that have expired - Do not store more than a 1 week supply of medicines in any workplace
Medical Equipment	- Medical equipment that has not been utilized for more than 1 year needs to be either disposed of or stored separately - Dispose of any out-of- order medical equipment

Figure 5.3 Examples of Disposal Criteria

PROCEDURES INVOLVED IN A DISPOSAL PROCESS

"Sort" must follow certain procedures until an item is thrown away by confirming that the item meets every criteria in order to be designated as unnecessary. Such procedures instruct the organization on how to deal with an item for which the final decision, as to whether it is truly necessary or not, is difficult to make. In any event, it is the organization's duty to make the final call and the organization should be held accountable for its actions and decisions.

Clearly identified procedures for judging items that are to be disposed of enable us to effectively respond to situations where additional unnecessary items are discovered, even after Clinical 5S is thoroughly implemented. This level of competency will also prevent future accumulation of unnecessary items in the workplace. Again, specific kinds of procedures have to be customized according to the unique situations of each hospital and working environment. I will describe a simplified example of necessary procedures in Figure 5.4.

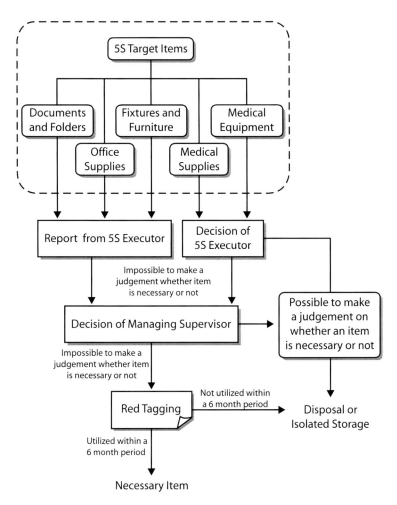

Figure 5.4 Example of Disposal Procedures

5-3 Red Tags

What are Red Tags?

Red Tags are attached to what are considered to be unnecessary items based upon "Sort" standards, and are used to finalize the judgement of whether an item is truly necessary or not.

Labeled items are collected in one place and are reviewed in order for us to conclude if they are necessary or not. Items that are finalized as unnecessary are logged on an "Unnecessary Item" list and are disposed of. The color of such labels is often red to make them stand out, therefore they are called "Red Labels" or "Red Tags."

Red Tag	
Item Name	
Quantity	
Tagged Date	
Date of Decision (Necessary or Unnecessary)	
Decision Maker	

Figure 5.5 Example of a Red Tag

How to judge if an item is necessary or unnecessary

Items are Sorted into necessary and unnecessary items according to the "Sort "disposal criteria. However, in many cases, such criteria may not be applicable to your work. You will need to find a way so that such criteria has meaning in the specific type of work you are responsible for, in order for you to make correct judgments. That is why the process of making an accurate final decision can be a quite time-consuming.

You may find "Sort" difficult to practice if you aim for perfection in doing so. My recommendation is to first classify items into 3 categories such as "absolutely unnecessary," "absolutely necessary," and "unclear." However, you will still have certain items that can belong to none of these categories. In such a case, items are temporarily stored, with Red Tags attached, and await a final decision after a specified period of time. A period of 6 months is generally used for this process.

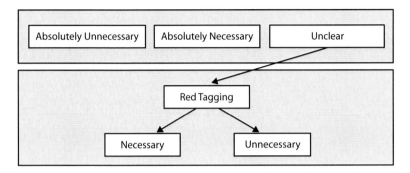

Figure 5.6 Example of Decision Making Process

CONTINUOUS PRACTICE OF "SORT"

As you practice Clinical 5S you will begin to experience a clutter-free workplace to a certain degree, with unnecessary items either eliminated or stored aside. However, if you cannot maintain a continuous practice of "Sort," your workplace will soon suffer again from an immediate accumulation of unnecessary items. There would be little added value to implementing Clinical 5S if "Sort" activities were only pursued tentatively for a short period of time. Therefore, it is extremely important to embed a mechanism to allow the application of "Sort" on a regular basis, and turn it into a habitual practice in each worker. I suggest that comprehensive "Sort" activities be carried out by hospitals once every 3 months in the early stage of Clinical 5S implementation. After the level of Clinical 5S improves dramatically within a hospital, I suggest twice a year. When Clinical 5S becomes well-established throughout the hospital, or a hospital becomes an expert at practicing Clinical 5S, I say once a year will be sufficient.

"Sort" has to be continuously executed on an individual level as well. To achieve this, each person must always clearly establish target areas for "Sort" and formulate action plans and schedules to be followed. For example, the frequency of an action can be determined for each target area, such as "desktops = daily," "inside of desks = once a month," "file cabinets = once every three months," and so forth. Most importantly, by following these rules and repeating the actions we will be able to internalize the importance of "Sort" and habitualize ourselves to practice "Sort" at a desired frequency.

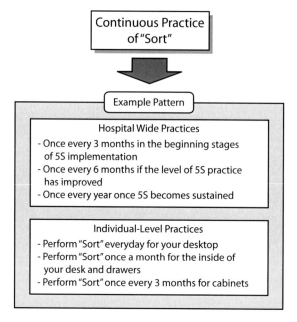

Figure 5.7 Continuous "Sort" Activities

5-4 Key Points in Implementing "Sort"

There are some key points to remember in order to implement "Sort" with a great level of certainty. They are as follows:

Key Point #1

Designate sufficient space for Sorted items to be stored.

In "Sort," the unnecessary items have to be gathered together in one location. If items are identified without a doubt as unnecessary they may as well be stored outside the hospital. However, often items that we deal with are not easy to distinguish as either necessary or unnecessary. That is why allocating sufficient space where such items can be temporality stored is necessary. In fact, our ability to secure such storage locations greatly influences the level of thoroughness that our Clinical 5S implementation can reach.

KEY POINT #2

Carry out "Sort" on a regular basis.

"Sort" is the very first activity to execute when adapting Clinical 5S. We need to remember here that "Sort" is not a one-time thing and should be repeated as a never-ending cycle. As you practice "Sort" continuously, the level of your skills for analyzing the condition of your workplace and effectively solving critical issues by utilizing "Sort" activities will greatly improve.

KEY POINT #3

Report to your superior if an item is too ambiguous to determine as necessary or not.

If you are capable of making the judgment by yourself, by all means go ahead. You should have proper disposal criteria and guidelines to comply with, which will help you make the right decision. However, if you are unable to do so, make sure you report the situation to your supervisors.

KEY POINT #4

Understand and reflect upon the fact that your failure to "Sort" items and documents around you implies that you are not capable of acknowledging the true way of Sorting your own responsibilities to complete the work given to you.

If items or documents around your desk or work area are always messy it is implied that you are confused as to how work should be performed, or you are simply disorganized in your head. It is absolutely impermissible to accept that hospitals, where human lives are at stake, continue to suffer from unnecessary items getting in the way of operations.

KEY POINT #5

Standards for "Sort" should continue to adjust.

If the fundamental criteria used to establish "Sort" standards changes, those standards have to be adjusted accordingly. For example, if unnecessary items are to be temporarily stored for 6 months, this storage duration can be changed to 4 months if found necessary.

Key Point #6

If "Set in Order" cannot be implemented in a thorough manner, it is because "Sort" is insufficiently practiced.

In many cases, many people have difficulties in ensuring "Set in Order" activities continue effectively. Many reasons for this can be considered, but the main possibility is that "Sort" has left things unfinished. If this is the case, "Set in Order" cannot be performed well, as appropriate places where items should be placed are not clearly identified. To solve this issue we need to revisit "Sort" and make sure that it has created a solid foundation for the next step.

Key Point #7

Workers should never waste their time in practicing "Sort." Instead, workers need to encourage themselves complete "Sort" at a fast pace.

The secret to successfully implementing "Sort" is to do it quickly and allow workers to have enough courage to dispose of items at their own will. This is because one ends up keeping an item if they are not completely sure whether or not the item is necessary or not. Therefore, if we want to succeed in "Sort," we need to make it a rule to eliminate items every time we find ourselves uncertain if the item is unnecessary or not.

CHAPTER 6
HOW TO IMPLEMENT "SET IN ORDER"

6-1 IMPLEMENTATION PROCEDURES FOR "SET IN ORDER"

THE BASIC PROCEDURES FOR ADAPTING "Set in Order" are as follows:

- Setting standards for "Set in Order" activities
- Defining the target areas for "Set in Order"
- Identifying issues with existing "Set in Order" methods
- Standardizing the way items are placed, locations where each item is placed, and how items are marked
- Consideration of practical implementation strategies and execution of "Set in Order"
- Evaluating results of "Set in Order" and seeking improvement ideas

In order to carry out "Set in Order" with certainty, it is also important to formulate a basic schedule for completing required actions and making sure that those actions are carried out at all times.

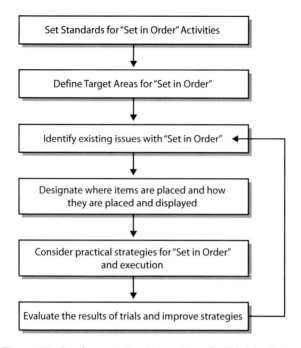

Figure 6.1 Implementation Procedures for "Set in Order"

At an early stage of implementing "Set in Order" it is also important for all of the Clinical 5S implementation members to collectively focus on fulfilling one specific objective of "Set in Order." This method allows implementation members across the hospital to have the same level of understanding toward "Set in Order" and their ways of executing "Set in Order" activities will become standardized as they continue to challenge and overcome issues together. After the level of competency among implementation members becomes well-balanced, each member is given an additional set of "Set in Order" objectives and is asked to concentrate on the workplace where they are responsible for adapting the "Set in Order" concept.

6-2 Setting Standards for "Set in Order" Activities

If "Set in Order" is expected to be implemented on the organizational level without having certain rules for labeling and placing items, the hospital will suffer from the lack of uniformity not only within a specific workplace but also among different workplaces in various departments. A workplace where the way of practicing "Set in Order" varies from one worker to another not only looks unattractive but is also difficult to work in.

On the other hand, imposing more rules than are necessary upon a workplace, in a uniform manner, can sometimes be problematic. It is important for us to respect the unique characteristics of each workplace and allow the creativity of each workplace to be reflected upon formulating desirable rules to follow. The degree of standardization should vary according to the unique circumstances of hospitals. However, I will describe the following rules as a minimum requirement that I recommend to all hospitals to standardize:

- Standardize the color of floor lining tape and the way it is displayed
- Items should not be placed directly on the floor
- Do not place anything on top of shelves and cabinets
- Standardize how and where labels are placed on shelves and cabinets
- Standardize how the binding edge of file folders are marked
- Remove wiring from the floor
- Leave nothing but a computer and telephone on the office desks during out of business hours

Needless to say, the common rules that I recommend are not limited to those above. Suggestions that reflect upon the distinctive characteristics of each workplaces should be submitted to the implementation committee and made into rules, if appropriate, so that the organization will be able to standardize "Set in Order" much more effectively across the board.

6-3 Defining the Target Areas for "Set in Order"
Prioritizing the target areas for "Set in Order"

Target areas signify the areas to which "Set in Order" should be adapted and a plan of action formulated. The important thing to remember here is that the successful and thorough implementation of "Set in Order" is strongly influenced by our ability to effectively prioritize target areas and allocate our efforts accordingly. The key in setting priorities for target areas is to put the highest priority on areas that are most likely to provide us with tangible results after "Set in Order" is applied. This method will bring your staff a great deal of reward for their continuous effort and reaffirm the true meaning of adapting Clinical 5S on the organization level.

The areas that can yield results in a relatively shorter time period should also be factored in when setting priorities on target areas. Areas that require a collective effort of implementation staff and areas where patients and customers are least fond of should receive higher priorities. To summarize, the list below are factors to be considered when prioritizing target areas for "Set in Order" activities.

- Areas where "Set in Order" can bring out the greatest results
- Areas where results can be gained in a relatively short period of time
- Areas that encourage a collective effort of implementation members
- Areas that your customers dislike or complain about

EXAMPLES OF TARGETED AREAS FOR "SET IN ORDER"

- Filing shelves and bookcases
- Cabinets containing documents
- Areas where X-ray negatives are stored
- Medical supply shelves
- Medicine shelves and medicine archive cabinets
- Information boards
- Areas where medical equipment is placed

6-4 SOLVING EXISTING ISSUES IN THE "SET IN ORDER" TARGET AREAS

EXISTING ISSUES WITH "SET IN ORDER" TARGET AREAS

Issues associated with the present condition of target areas have to be clearly identified so that our continuous improvement ideas for each target area can effectively address the true objectives. In other words, it is important to acknowledge what aspects of a target area that staff are having problems with in the first place. Then appropriate continuous improvement strategies should be considered accordingly, in order to address each outstanding issue.

It is important to remember that Clinical 5S is an effective approach to problem solving. Implementing Clinical 5S in a thorough manner allows us to identify and resolve critical issues typically found in a workplace. I have run into many cases where Clinical 5S is treated as an ultimate goal. However, in these cases, the purpose and method are reversed in such a manner that hospitals are attempting to adapt Clinical 5S only for the sake of Clinical 5S. I cannot stress enough that the existing issues that workers are suffering from, and guidelines to follow for performing the right work, have to be clearly identified first, with an understanding that Clinical 5S is solely an effective tool for problem solving.

REAL ISSUES ARE THE GAP BETWEEN THE IDEAL SITUATION AND REALITY

A question like "What are the key issues?" seems like a simple question but it is often difficult to answer. I equate the key existing issues to the gap between the ideal situation and reality. As for "Set in Order," ideal situations will be conditions where "Sort" and "Set in Order" are thoroughly adapted to make our work as easy as possible to perform. The gap between these conditions and reality is the primary issue that we must concentrate upon first.

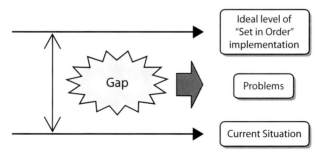

Figure 6.2 Problems of "Set in Order"

6-5 IMPORTANCE OF 3 RULES IN "SET IN ORDER"

FOLLOWING THE 3 FUNDAMENTAL RULES OF "SET IN ORDER"

Improving the level of "Set in Order" implementation requires us to approach problem solving with a clear understanding of the 3 significant rules of "Set in Order," as well as integrate an effective mechanism to ensure that items are always returned to their locations, as designated by "Set in Order." The 3 fundamental rules for "Set in Order" that must always be complied with are as follows:

RULE 1

Areas where items need to be placed are clearly designated and displayed.

RULE 2

How items need to be placed is clearly defined.

RULE 3

Both every item and the locations where items need to be placed are clearly labeled.

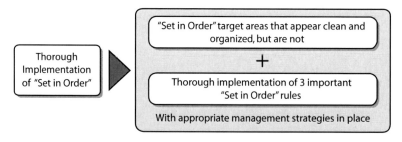

Figure 6.3 Importance of the 3 Rules of "Set in Order"

A truly well-managed "Set in Order" is one where these 3 rules are clearly defined and followed at all times. A workplace where everything looks clean and organized does not mean that "Set in Order" is thoroughly implemented. The key is to reach a point where we are able to manage how "Set in Order" is administered to ensure true implementation.

6-6 FUNDAMENTAL RULES BEHIND DESIGNATING WHERE ITEMS SHOULD BE PLACED

The first rule of the 3 "Set in Order" rules is to clearly identify certain places where items need to be stored. I will explain some key points to follow in this process.

1. Every single item is given a designated location for placement.

   As a general rule, every item found in a hospital is given a placement location. For example, items like wheelchairs and intravenous stands are assigned specific storage locations after use. Items that are often used on a medical table need to be put back in a designated spot as well.

2. Define fixed locations and quantities of items to store.

   A fixed location means that each item is to be stored in the same place at all times. Fixed quantity means that each item is to be stored in a specified amount at all times. Both a maximum allowed quantity and a minimum allowed quantity have to be indicated for every location where items are placed.

3. Choose a location for each item to maximize efficiency.

   Locations need to be selected according to the frequency of use for each item and in a manner that minimizes wasteful operations as much as possible. Items that we use frequently should be placed nearby and vice versa. For storing items on shelves, heavier items should be stored on a lower level to allow easier access.

4. Optimal space where each item is stored can be flexibly adjusted.

   We need to be able to manage placement locations of items in a resilient manner. When items run out of space to be stored in, we need to ensure that additional space can be flexibly reallocated to accommodate any changes.

6-7 FUNDAMENTAL RULES OF PLACING ITEMS

The second rule of "Set in Order" is to specify how items should be placed. Not having proper rules not only creates a disorganized workplace by sight but also requires workers to spend more time searching for necessary items, as well as causing them to make various other mistakes.

1. Place items in either a parallel or perpendicular manner.

   Items should be placed either parallel or perpendicular to the wall and marking tape should be on the floor. Following this fundamental principle gives out a sense of well-established management as well as an aesthetic appreciation toward your workplace.

2. Place items so that they can easily be retrieved.

   It is important to place items so that you can find and extract them easily. For example, an item should be placed with its name label facing toward you. Otherwise much time will be wasted in trying to identify the item and a wrong item can be retrieved instead, which will cause other serious errors. Nurse stations and examinations rooms especially, which deal with many different types of medicines, require our attention in this respect.

3. Items should not go over designated boundaries.

   It is important to keep an item within its designated boundaries at all times. We need to pay particular attention to items that are to be stored in hallways. Items that go over their boundaries in hallways will not only get in the way of pedestrians but also can lead to many serious safety issues when colliding with patients.

4. Continuously improve the way items are placed.

   The way items are placed has a great deal of impact upon the efficiency and safety of workers when they attempt to retrieve items. It is important to continuously improve how we place items so that your workplace not only looks organized, but also benefits from a higher level of efficiency.

6-8 FUNDAMENTAL RULES OF LABELING

The third rule of the "Set in Order" rules is to standardize how items are labeled. Labeling is equally as important as designating areas of placement and specifying how items are to be placed.

1. Follow the "Item : Location = 1 : 1" rule.

   Every single item is given a label that corresponds to the one attached to its designated location. This ensures all items will be returned to their unique placement location at all times by matching labels.

2. Standardize how items are labeled.

   The basic rule is to apply the same method of labeling items across the hospital. In particular, the following items need to be standardized first:

   • Labels on the binding side of file folders (standardize display items, font type, font size, layout, etc.)

   • The kind of marking tape to be used to identify access aisles, placement locations for stretchers, wheelchairs, medical carts, etc.

   • Labels to be attached to file cabinets (label content, label display method, and location where labels are attached)

   • Label color (for documents, medicines, medical supplies, etc.)

3. Continuously improve how items are labeled.

   The following aspects of the way items are labeled should be continuously improved:

   • Find an easier way to change the content of a label

   • Make a better use of color coding

6-9 METHODS OF LABELING
FOLLOW THE "ITEM : LOCATION = 1 : 1 RULE"

The basic rule of thumb is to give one label to every single item and one corresponding label, with an identical description, to the location where an item needs to be stored. This is called the "Item : Location = 1 : 1 Rule," which ensures that items can always be returned to their designated placement locations. If placement locations need to change after a short period of time I recommended using magnetic labels so that labels can be transferred easily.

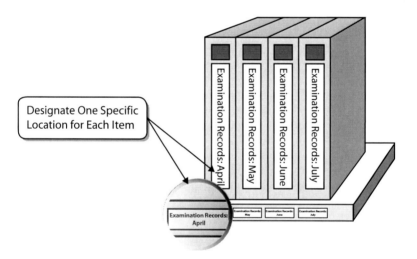

Figure 6.4 Item to Location is 1:1 Ratio

INDICATE A GROUP NAME ON THE PLACEMENT LOCATION AND GIVE A CORRESPONDING ID LABEL TO THE ITEM

When items are hard to be identified using the "Item : Location = 1 : 1 Rule," or the rule itself is difficult to adapt, we can label placement locations with their group names and give each item a corresponding group ID. This way items can be matched with group labels at the placement locations.

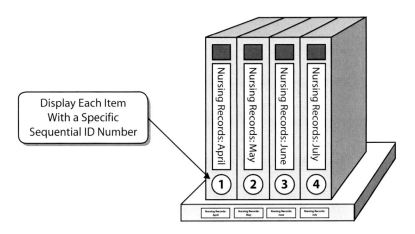

Figure 6.5 Using ID Numbers for Labeling

LABELING METHOD FOR DIVIDING SHELF SPACE

Shelves can be divided by using partition panels or marking tape.

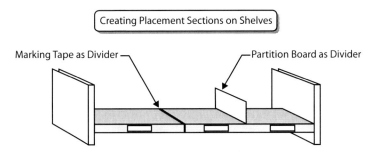

Figure 6.6 Dividing Shelves into Sections

LABELING METHOD FOR THE BINDING SIDE OF FILE FOLDERS

The way the binding side of folders is labeled, as well as its given description, needs to be standardized across the hospital. This type of overall uniformity allows for a more effective management structures and leads to an increased aesthetic value of a workplace. If file folders were simply given traditional, generic word-processed labels, it would not only make a workplace appear unattractive to work in, but also indicate that a poor quality of management is in place.

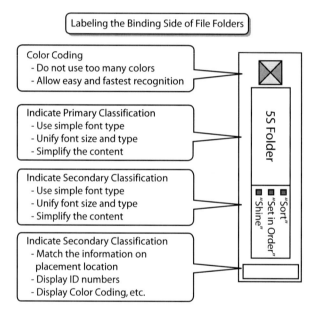

Figure 6.7 Proper Labeling of File Folders

Labeling method for shelves and cabinets

Please refer to Figure 6.8 for required label specifications as well as locations where labels need to be attached.

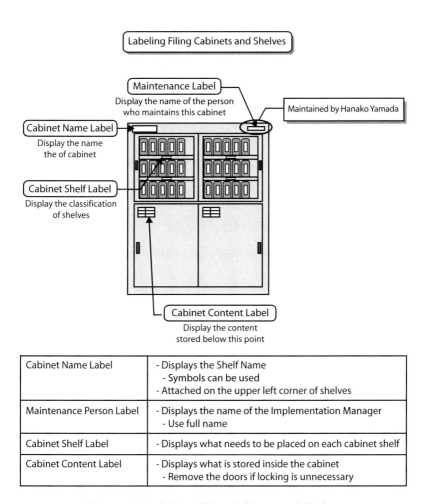

Cabinet Name Label	- Displays the Shelf Name - Symbols can be used - Attached on the upper left corner of shelves
Maintenance Person Label	- Displays the name of the Implementation Manager - Use full name
Cabinet Shelf Label	- Displays what needs to be placed on each cabinet shelf
Cabinet Content Label	- Displays what is stored inside the cabinet - Remove the doors if locking is unnecessary

Figure 6.8 Labeling Filing Cabinets and Shelves

6-10 Case Studies for Implementing the 3 Rules of "Set in Order"

How Items Should Be Placed in Drawers

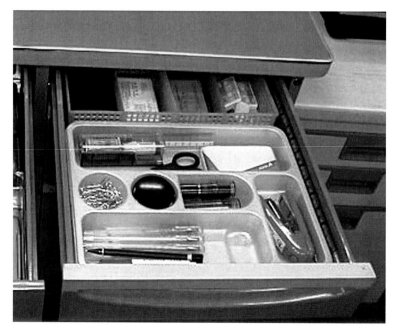

Photo 6.1 Inside of a Drawer #1

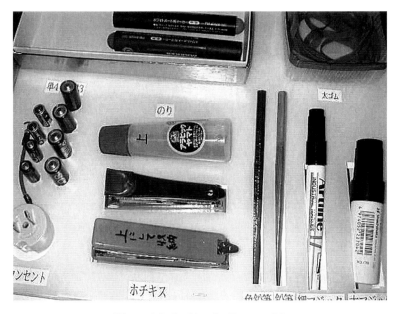

Photo 6.2 Inside of a Drawer #2

BENEFITS

- Items can be searched quickly and immediately
- Items can be returned to original placement locations
- Immediately know when an item is missing
- Items can be replenished if necessary
- It makes it harder to place wrong items into the drawer
- The drawer has a good, clean physical appearance

METHOD USED

- Photo 6.1 Store-bought products (drawer organizers) are used
- Photo 6.2 Shapes of the items are cut out so that items can be inserted into fixed positions in Photo

CREATING CUSTOM HOLDERS

Common items such as office supplies, which many workers frequently share amongst one another, need to be placed to ensure that items are always returned to fixed locations. As indicated in the case study below, one effective way is to create custom holders for each item in their specific shape.

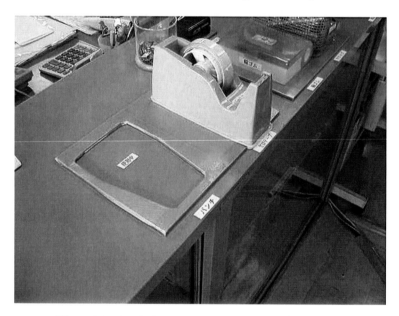

Photo 6.3 Fixed Placement of Common Office Supplies

BENEFITS

- Wrong items cannot be placed
- Items can be returned to designated locations with ease
- Items can only be placed in the correct way

METHOD USED

- A sheet of foam material is cut out according to the unique shapes of items to be placed inside, then the cutout sheet is attached to cabinets
- Each cutout part is clearly labeled to indicate what item is to be placed inside

"Set in Order" for small objects

For items such as thermometers and keys, which can often be scattered around easily, movable holders can be created and are put back to designated locations after use. (Photo 6.4)

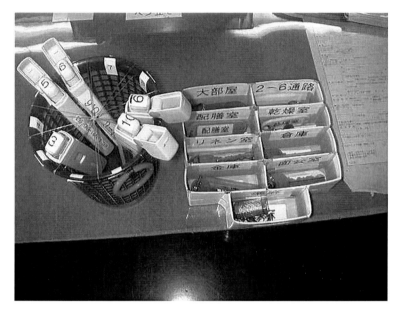

Photo 6.4 "Set in Order" for Small Items

Benefits

- Prevent items from scattering around
- Items can be easily returned to where they were retrieved from a movable holder
- Movable holders can easily be returned to designated locations after use

Method used

- Store-bought containers can be divided into smaller sections
- Small boxes are put together to create compartments for keys to be placed in
- Each compartment is clearly labeled for specific items to return to
- Movable holders are always returned to specified placement locations

"SET IN ORDER" MEDICAL SUPPLY ITEMS

Storage cases are customized to place small medical supply items inside.

Photo 6.5 Placement Example for Medical Supply Items

BENEFITS

- Items can be stored in a compactible way
- Items can be retrieved easily
- Color coding prevents wrong items from being picked out

METHOD USED

- A number of empty intravenous plastic bottles are used to create the storage device
- Bottle caps are color coded
- There is no additional cost for supplies (however, production time is required)

PREPARING INTRAVENOUS SUPPLIES FOR DIFFERENT PATIENTS

There are many cases where staff in a hospital have mistakenly taken wrong intravenous supplies to patients, as they simply prepared the supplies on a medical table without any guidelines to follow. To prevent this type of risk once and for all, the way in which intravenous supplies are prepared is standardized across the hospital by utilizing bookends in a creative way.

Photo 6.6 "Standardizing" Intravenous Supplies

BENEFITS

- The surfaces of medical tables can be "Set in Order"
- Intravenous supplies can be prepared for one patient at a time, which prevents mistakes — especially when staff is on a tight time schedule
- Bookends can be returned to designated locations after preparation is complete, which allows a high degree of usability

METHOD USED

- Store-bought bookends are labeled with the ID number of patient rooms
- I.V. bottles are placed next to corresponding bookends
- Bookends are returned to the designated placement locations after use

MEDICINE SHELVES

Each shelf is clearly labeled for a specific medicine to be placed upon. Also, the rule that items are always placed in parallel and perpendicular manners should be enforced at all times.

Photo 6.7 "Set in Order" for Medicine Shelves

BENEFITS

- All medicine is placed at a fixed location
- Inventory status of all medicines can be learned easily
- Prevents wrong medicines from being picked out

METHOD USED

- Labels containing specific names of medicines are attached to placement locations, found on each shelf
- Make it a rule to place medicines in a way that their labels can be easily seen from the front of the shelves

6-11 Considerations for Implementing "Set in Order"

Practical guideline considerations

Prior to executing "Set in Order" activities, effective and specific implementation instructions have to be considered by following the common guidelines for formulating practical "Set in Order" strategies. In principle, such instructions are established separately for every single target area.

Practical instructions are to be considered by both the Clinical 5S leader and implementation members in a collective manner. This process allows the participants to acknowledge what it means to implement Clinical 5S in the correct way and helps them generate many effective implementation methodologies.

Please refer to Figure 6.9 for an actual plan of action that is based upon the common guidelines for formulating practical "Set in Order" strategies.

"Set in Order" Practical Guideline Consideration Sheet

"Set in Order" Practical Guideline Consideration Procedures
1. Select one target area for "Set in Order"
2. List existing issues with the target area
3. Consider "Set in Order" objective strategy
4. Visualize actual implementation (diagram)
5. Describe Key Points/Guidelines to follow

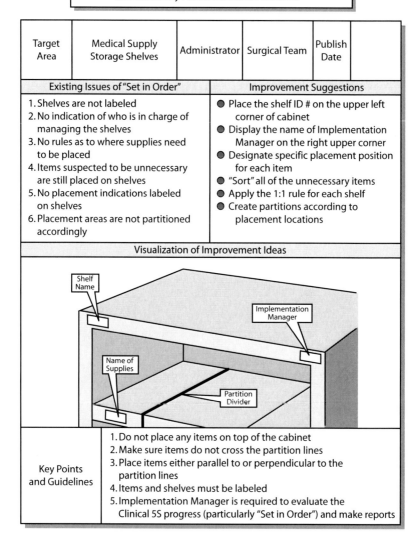

Target Area	Medical Supply Storage Shelves	Administrator	Surgical Team	Publish Date	

Existing Issues of "Set in Order"	Improvement Suggestions
1. Shelves are not labeled 2. No indication of who is in charge of managing the shelves 3. No rules as to where supplies need to be placed 4. Items suspected to be unnecessary are still placed on shelves 5. No placement indications labeled on shelves 6. Placement areas are not partitioned accordingly	● Place the shelf ID # on the upper left corner of cabinet ● Display the name of Implementation Manager on the right upper corner ● Designate specific placement position for each item ● "Sort" all of the unnecessary items ● Apply the 1:1 rule for each shelf ● Create partitions according to placement locations

Visualization of Improvement Ideas

Shelf Name

Implementation Manager

Name of Supplies

Partition Divider

Key Points and Guidelines	1. Do not place any items on top of the cabinet 2. Make sure items do not cross the partition lines 3. Place items either parallel to or perpendicular to the partition lines 4. Items and shelves must be labeled 5. Implementation Manager is required to evaluate the Clinical 5S progress (particularly "Set in Order") and make reports

Figure 6.9 "Set in Order" Practical Guideline Consideration Sheet

6-12 Key Points in Implementing "Set in Order"

It is true to say that "Set in Order" takes the most amount of time for us to improve upon, as far as necessary Clinical 5S activities are concerned. Unless we can confidently say that "Set in Order" principles are fully integrated into our daily operations, our overall Clinical 5S implementation efforts will most likely continue to fail. Keep in mind the following key points when adapting the "Set in Order" principles in order to ensure its success.

Key Point #1

100% designation of placement locations.

As far as "Set in Order" is concerned, absolutely all of the areas targeted by Clinical 5S must be allocated for the placment of specific items and must be clearly labeled for their corresponding items 100% of the time. The key point here is the 100% — no exceptions are allowed as the basic rule. It is extremely important to clearly identify what every single placement location is meant for. In other words, there will be no scenarios where you fail to understand where specific items have to be stored in any target area.

Key Point #2

Visualize how a workplace should look after "Set in Order."

Another effective way for putting "Set in Order" implementation tactics into practice is to draw out how you desire a workplace to look like after "Set in Order" is fully adapted. This process of determining an ideal "Set in Order" model puts you back in the right direction for coming up with more appropriate strategies, as well as providing the entire team with additional educational opportunities to revisit the true meaning of "Standardize." Upon agreeing on the ideal model, a careful preparation, including taking into consideration the appropriate key points, becomes necessary.

It is often expected that you will run into many obstacles when executing your plan of action, therefore the resolutions for overcoming such challenges have to be discussed in this preparation stage as well. Here we can utilize the guidelines for formulating practical "Set in Order" strategies in order to visualize what the future should look like and formulate strategies to achieve that goal.

Key Point #3

The way items should be "Set in Order" has to be formulated with the involvement of those who are actually using the items.
As described in Key Point #2, the process of deciding on an ideal model for each workplace should closely reflect the opinions of those who operate in such a workplace. This is an effective method to ensure that the implementation of "Set in Order" in target places is effective, and motivates participating workers to try harder at achieving better results in practice than what is expected.

Key Point #4

Clearly identify the common rules to be followed throughout the hospital as a minimum requirement.
Common rules that are set for the entire hospital to follow should, of course, be applied to implementing "Set in Order." Following such rules persistently will significantly refine the results of "Set in Order."

Key Point #5

If "Set in Order" activities get off track or lose focus, find the underlying cause and resolve the issue immediately.
Even if we can maintain a thorough implementation of "Set in Order" for a certain time period, things can still get out of balance somewhere down the line. When this happens it is extremely important to not only put everything back to normal but also to analyze the true cause of a problem so that the same mistakes will not reoccur. The worst thing you can do is to leave out-of-balance "Set in Order" activities alone. The negative effects would most likely spread across the entire organization.

KEY POINT #6

Implementation rules and guidelines must be followed at all times.

Whether or not Clinical 5S can be adapted thoroughly is heavily dependent upon how well every worker can internalize the implementation rules and guidelines. Therefore, the importance of education and effective guidance for workers must be emphasized here, and such training has to be conducted repeatedly until we can ensure that each worker reaches a desired competency level. We also need to train ourselves to be patient and persistent, as this is a time-consuming process.

KEY POINT #7

Utilize available tools for "Set in Order" in the most effective manner possible.

As I described thus far, there are many useful tools we can utilize to implement "Set in Order." It is critical for us to make sure that these tools are always applied in the most effective manner possible as well as continue to develop other innovative tools that are customized to work with the unique situations of your organization.

CHAPTER 7
"SHINE"

7-1 IMPLEMENTATION PROCEDURES FOR "SHINE"

"SHINE" ACTIVITIES ARE IMPLEMENTED BY following certain steps, as described below:

1. Set tentative standards for "Shine."
2. Carry out a collective "Shine" activity across the entire organization.
3. Through this cleaning, identify problems and formulate continuous improvement strategies.
4. Identify responsibilities and perform role-sharing for "Shine" as well as setting practical methods for cleaning.
5. Continue to carry out "Shine" activities on a regular basis and confirm the progress of implementation.

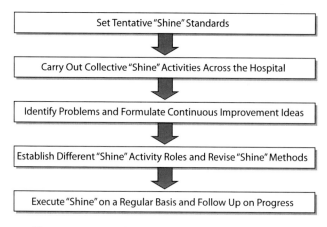

Figure 7.1 Procedures for "Shine" Implementation

An Important aspect of "Shine" is to acknowledge that "Shine" is a much more thorough activity than regular cleaning activities from the past. It is also different in the respect that the full participation of your staff is required in order to ensure successful implementation. To achieve this, a set of standards for "Shine" must be established as guidelines for cleaning. Such standards should be set tentatively at first and modified throughout performing the actual "Shine" activities, until they can be designated as official rules to follow in the future.

7-2 COLLECTIVE "SHINE" ACTIVITY

WHAT IS A COLLECTIVE "SHINE" ACTIVITY?

A collective "Shine" activity takes place with the full participation of staff in a simultaneous manner across the organization. In this activity, out-of-reach areas that do not get cleaned on a regular basis are to be swept out. Doing this allows us to gather basic information that can be used for establishing appropriate methods of "Shine" and divide responsibilities among the team members. Critical information, used for solving problematic areas in a focused way, can be collected through carrying out this comprehensive "Shine" activity.

Procedures for organizing a collective "Shine" activity

Important steps for implementing a collective "Shine" activity are as follows:

1. Set the target area for a collective "Shine" activity in each workplace.

2. Establish an outline for how responsibilities are shared in the workplace.

3. Define tentative responsibilities for commonly-used areas that have not been cleaned before.

4. Set a date and time duration for the activity.

5. Perform necessary preparation for executing the activity.

   – Prepare guidelines for solving problem areas.

   – Prepare applications for submitting problem areas.

   – Confirm the availability and condition of cleaning tools.

   – Adapt the purpose and method of the activity in a thorough manner.

7-3 Continuously Improve Problem Areas

Many problems associated with the condition of medical facilities and hospital buildings themselves can be pointed out in the process of carrying out a collective "Shine" activity. It is important to establish a set of rules for solving such indicated problems. As a general rule at this point, each hospital should make clear, and effectively utilize, the pre-established procedures for requesting continuous improvement initiatives for problem areas. For your reference, I will describe an example of a "Continuous Improvement Initiative Form" to be used for requesting assistance in solving problems found during the course of conducting a collective "Shine" activity. The content of problems are to be described on the form, which will be submitted to an appropriate department for continuous improvement expertise.

Continuous Improvement Initiative Form					
Department	X-ray dept.	Name	Taro Yamada	Request Date	5/01/09
Problem Area	Description			Solution	Manager in Charge
Floor	Some tiles are coming off the floor			Replacing tiles	Mr. Yamashita
Wall	Holes in the wall			Restoring the wall	Mr. Tokunaga

Improvement Execution Schedule Report Form				
Problem Area	Administrator	Action Plan	Action Execution Date	Improvement Area
Floor	Mr. Tanaka	Replacing tiles	5/01/09	Floor
Wall	Mr. Tanaka	Restoring the wall	5/01/09	Wall

Figure 7.2 Continuous Improvement Forms

7-4 SHARING THE RESPONSIBILITIES OF "SHINE"

As far as "Shine" is concerned, it is important to clearly identify "By Who," "Where," "When," and "How" each cleaning activity should be carried out. Management representatives who are designated to be responsible for managing both "Sort" and "Set in Order" are basically required to manage "Shine" activities as well. However, it does not mean that they are responsible for performing all of the cleaning.

We need to pay special attention to the places that are communally-used, such as lunchrooms. Everyone often wonders who is in charge of cleaning such places, which slows down the process of "Shine" implementation in a significant way. To prevent the problem of having such uncertain areas, every single area of the hospital must be assigned to a responsible person to carry out "Shine."

ESTABLISH THE SHARING OF ROLES AND METHODS FOR "SHINE"

Sharing of roles and methods for "Shine" should be tentatively determined based upon the current actual achievement, while taking into consideration the responsibilities of each staff member toward work itself. Then a collective "Shine" activity is carried out according to preliminary shared roles and methods, which are to be repeatedly reviewed. This process is basically how standards for "Shine" can be established.

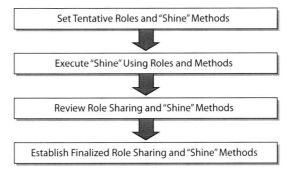

Figure 7.3 Establishing Role Sharing and Methods for "Shine"

7-5 Standards for "Shine"

What are the standards for "Shine"?

The standards for "Shine" are a set of rules by which cleaning activities in a workplace are to be executed, on a regular basis. Such standards are later solidified based upon both the tentative guidelines established for an initial collective "Shine" activity and the actual results of collective "Shine" activities.

"Shine" standards ensure that a workplace receives a cleaning on a regular basis and are effective tools for maintaining the cleanliness. It is safe to say that there would not be any positive results if our cleaning activities did not follow the "Shine" standards. Therefore, an accurate analysis of "Shine" standards is extremely critical and must be conducted in a way that the initial "Shine" standards can consistently and practically be improved upon and executed by employees. It is when staff members gradually gain more experience that "Shine" standards can require more improved and sophisticated responsibilities from each person. In addition, effective Visual Management tools, such as calendars signifying plans of action based on "Shine" standards, can be implemented.

Procedures for establishing "Shine" standards

As I have described thus far, a set of preliminary standards should be set first and should be reviewed repeatedly after executing collective "Shine" activities in order to solidify more appropriate official "Shine" standards for the whole organization. The followings are some key points to take into consideration when formulating "Shine" standards.

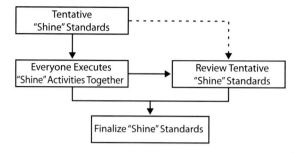

Figure 7.4 Procedures for Setting "Shine" Standards

KEY POINTS FOR ESTABLISHING "SHINE" STANDARDS

- "Shine" standards have to be executable
- "Shine" standards have to be based on full participation
- "Shine" standards have to be persuading to every staff member
- "Shine" standards have to be adjusted in a flexible manner according to changing conditions

REQUIREMENTS FOR ESTABLISHING "SHINE" STANDARDS

- Where? — Target areas
- How? — Methods of cleaning
- Level of sophistication? — Extent of cleaning
- Who? — Person in charge of cleaning a specific target area
- Timing? — Frequency of "Shine" execution
- How long? — Duration of each "Shine" activity

		Creation Date	Group Name	Manager	Prepared and Monitored by:
"Shine" Standards		3/5/2004	Team Members:	Yoneyama	Saito
			Saito, Yamamoto, Takigawa, Okabe		

No.	Target Area	"Shine" Standards (What? / Intensity?)	"Shine" Method (How?)	Executor	Duration	"Shine" Frequency		
						Mo.	Week	Day
1	Trash and Dust on the floor	Dust cannot be seen	Dust removed by Mopping and Vacuuming	Takigawa	5 min			①
2	Trash and Dust on Medical Table	Dust cannot be seen and hands stay clean when touching Medical tables	Scrubbing with wet cloth and vacuuming	Takigawa	5 min		①	
3	Trash and Dust under beds	Dust cannot be seen and hands stay clean when touching	Mopping and Vacuuming	Okabe	10 min		②	
4	Trash and Dust on shelves	Dust cannot be seen	Wipe with wet cloth or scrubbing rag	Okabe	5 min			

This means "to execute twice a week."

Figure 7.5 Examples of "Shine" Standards

CREATE CALENDARS TO REMIND OF SCHEDULED "SHINE" ACTIVITIES

"Shine" standards by themselves cannot ensure that cleaning is always carried out as required. Unless the person in charge of each daily cleaning responsibility is clearly indicated, as shown in Figure 7.5, we tend to forget performing necessary responsibilities as scheduled, especially those that occur irregularly such as once a week or twice a month. To solve this problem we can consider creating what is referred to as "Shine" Calendars at the beginning of each month, which are based upon the requirements defined by "Shine" standards and with which we can remind ourselves of the "When," "By Who," and "Where" factors on a daily basis.

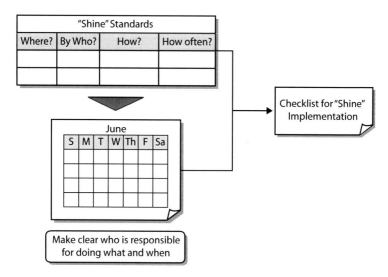

Figure 7.6 Creating Schedules and Calendars for "Shine" Activities

In addition, we need an effective method of confirming that each one of the responsibilities was executed as planned. Clearly outlined checklists should be implemented in practice and monitored on a regular basis by the person in charge of managing 5S activities.

7-6 KEY POINTS FOR "SHINE" IMPLEMENTATION

KEY POINT #1

Clearly defined role-sharing is extremely important.

As you already know, "Shine" is a continuous activity, and the full participation of your staff is the minimum requirement, which makes it critical to clearly identify in advance the responsibilities of each team and the specific roles of every single person involved.

However, the least desirable situation would be when your staff begins having a sense of unfairness after learning that some people are given less or more cleaning responsibilities than others. This type of negativity among workers will quickly spread across the organization and pose a serious risk to future implementation efforts of Clinical 5S. Last but not least, management-level staff should also be given cleaning responsibilities to perform.

KEY POINT #2

A mechanism to allow regular monitoring of all "Shine" executions is a must.

After "Shine" standards are established we need to have a monitoring system in place to be able to make sure that each necessary activity is executed regularly, as outlined by such standards. We do not have to do anything elaborate for this purpose, simply create checklists that allows us to check off the necessary activities after completion.

KEY POINT #3

Eliminate the cause of dirtiness and the originating point of trash by continuous improvement.

The more we determine that "Shine" needs to be implemented in a thorough manner, the more of our time and effort will be required. Even though we continue to spend our resources to ensure that "Shine" activities comply with the set standards at all times, a comprehensive implementation of "Shine" does not always directly result in an increased level of productivity of our operations.

This is the reason we need to use our ideas; so that the

amount of time spent cleaning to maintain the cleanliness of a workplace can be greatly minimized. Eliminating the cause of dirtiness and the originating point of trash, as much as possible, is an effective way of reducing the frequency of cleaning and the amount of time required. When a source is discovered, you should immediately generate strategies for achieving goals such as "reduce or destroy the source completely," "prevent littering from the source," and so on.

KEY POINT #4

Continuously improve challenging areas where "Shine" needs to be carried out.

It is important to continuously improve challenging areas in order to implement "Shine" in a thorough manner and to reduce the time required to execute various "Shine" activities. Some examples of such continuous improvement ideas may include lifting wiring off the floor to perform cleaning duties easier and creating customized cleaning tools for areas that cannot be reached by ordinary cleaning tools.

Chapter 8

How to Maintain "Standardize" in a Workplace

8-1 "Standardize" in a Workplace and Visual Management

How to create a "Standardized" workplace

By definition, "Standardize" is a "condition in which cleanliness is well-maintained in a workplace at all times." Therefore, in a practical sense, it is extremely critical to consider how we can effectively manage maintaining such a condition.

What is primarily required to manage the 3S's ("Sort," "Set in Order," and "Shine") is the formulation of rules for "Standardization." Then Visual Management tools have to be implemented so that we can determine whether or not such rules and standards are always followed. The ability to visually assess the level of management in a workplace is also an effective tool for maintaining cleanliness. Let me explain here how to promote Visual Management for making a clean environment in the workplace.

What is Visual Management?

I define Visual Management as "a mechanism or methodology that allows us to precisely 'see' how things are running in practice and react to the current situation with appropriate judgment and actions in a timely manner." In other words, the issues and abnormalities associated with a workplace can be immediately identified by sight and effective solutions can be applied for improvement. This ability alone is sufficient to justify why Clinical 5S needs to be implemented. For example, certain mechanisms have to be adapted so that we are able to prepare intravenous supplies correctly, identify an abnormality when an item protrudes into the hallway, and immediately correct mistakes when they are made.

Figure 8.1 Effectiveness of Visual Management

When we reach a point where we begin benefiting from Clinical 5S for identifying problems and abnormalities in the workplace we can say that Visual Management has been established for the purpose of maintaining a "Standardized" work environment.

8-2 Important Aspects of Visual Management

4 Aspects of Visual Management

4 important aspects of Visual Management are visualization, clarification, marking, and sharing rules.

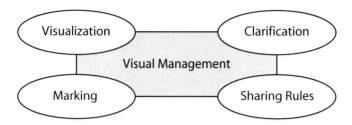

Figure 8.2 Key Aspects of Visual Management

"Visualization" allows you to see the condition of work and the workplace itself. In order to adapt "visualization" we can use many techniques, such as using transparent containers, color coding items, or diagraming the necessary steps in a process.

"Clarification" helps us draw appropriate judgments and actions by eliminating any ambiguity that is found in a workplace. Color coding, as well as identifying items by numbers and symbols, are effective tools for "clarification."

"Marking" allows us to identify items in a precise manner and trigger necessary actions to perform for each item. Some examples are marking items uniquely, drawing guide lines, and applying an indexing system to items.

"Sharing of Rules" creates an environment where workers can effectively share important guidelines about how work should be completed. Sharing such critical information eliminates inconsistency among how each worker performs an operation and, as a result, stabilizes the overall operation.

"Visualization"

Effective methods for realizing "visualization" concepts incorporate such elements as utilizing transparency, creating diagrams, marking items, color coding, graphing statistics, and using a Kanban System.

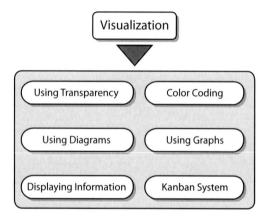

Figure 8.3 Visualization Methods

Utilizing Transparency
- Use transparent containers so that the inside is visible
- Create peeking windows so that the inside can be seen
- Use removable doors so that, when opened, the inside can be seen

Creating Diagrams
- Map out operational procedures in a diagram format so that it can be understood by sight
- Utilize a diagram to indicate shared "Shine" responsibilities in a clear manner

Color Coding
- Medicines are color coded and stored based on their color designation
- Color code the binding side of file folders for easier identification
- Color code the existing hospital information boards and signs

Graphing Statistics
- Visually indicate the seriousness of human errors by graphing the statistical information of mistakes that have occurred
- Visually indicate the seriousness of wasted time by graphing how much time is required to look for certain items

Using a Kanban System
- Avoid ordering mistakes by utilizing a Kanban System for ordering both office and medical supplies

"CLARIFICATION"

Effective methods for realizing the "clarification" concept incorporate such elements as assigning ID numbers, assigning ID symbols, color coding, and making clear the placement boundaries.

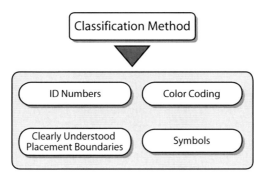

Figure 8.4 Classification Methods

Assigning ID Numbers
- Assign ID numbers to file folders so they are always returned to designated locations
- Assign ID numbers to intravenous stands so they are always returned to designated locations
- Assign ID numbers to different steps of work based on the sequence so that it can be performed in an accurate manner

Assigning Symbols
- Assign symbols to shelves so that items can be searched for easily

- Assigning symbols allows us to classify items for a better way of organization

Color Coding
- Medicines are color coded and stored based on their color designation
- Color code the binding side of file folders for easier identification
- Color code the existing hospital information boards and signs

Making Clear the Placement Boundaries
- Utilize floor marking tape to define placement areas in order to avoid mixing items
- Clearly distinguish placement locations for clean and dirty items

"MARKING"

Effective methods for realizing "marking" concept incorporate such elements as spotting, drawing reference lines, and indexing.

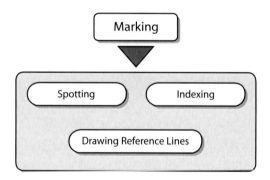

Figure 8.5 Marking Methods

Spotting
- Put measurement marks on containers to help fill up the contents without errors
- Put marks on the gauge of measuring devices, such as a weighing machine, which allows one to determine whether or not the device is functioning accurately

Drawing Reference Lines
- Draw reference lines to clearly identify where items, such as stretchers, have to be placed in order to ensure safety
- Draw reference lines to make it easier for patients to stand in line without confusion

Indexing
- Index file folders so that they can be searched easily
- Index medical charts so that they can be searched in an efficient manner

"Sharing of Rules"

Effective methods for realizing the "sharing of rules" concept incorporate such elements as unification of rules, putting into rules, standardization of rules, and the posting of rules. Here I will combine and consider unification of rules, putting into rules, and the standardization of rules as one concept.

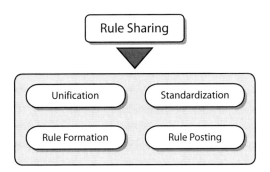

Figure 8.6 Rule Sharing Methods

Unification of rules, putting into rules, and the standardization of rules
- Unify the display colors used across the hospital
- Unify and make into rules the font type and size to be displayed on the binding sides of file folders
- Unify and standardize the content and location of information attached on shelves and cabinets
- Make into rules how "Sort" activities should be executed

- Make into rules how "Shine" activities should be executed and how responsibilities are to be shared among team members

Posting of rules

- Post content that is unified and made into rules in a way that everyone can share at a glance
- Post by using photographs to demonstrate rules and to show how each item needs to be placed
- Make into rules and post information related to how each medical device should be used (a manual)

8-3 EXAMPLES OF VISUAL MANAGEMENT
EXAMPLE 1: MANAGING THE TIMING AT WHICH SUPPLIES
SHOULD BE ORDERED

Figure 8.7 is an example of a mechanism with which we can notify ourselves when certain items need to be restocked, or ordered, by studying reference (ordering) points that have been previously marked. Each storage case should have an elongated hole in it, which will allow us to discern the existing volume of content inside. Also, alongside the hole, there should be a reference point marked, which signifies the point of ordering and triggers the appropriate action to perform necessary ordering or restocking activities.

Visual Management principles used in this example are:

- Visualization — using transparency and color coding
- Marking — spotting and drawing reference lines
- Sharing of rules — putting into rules and posting of rules

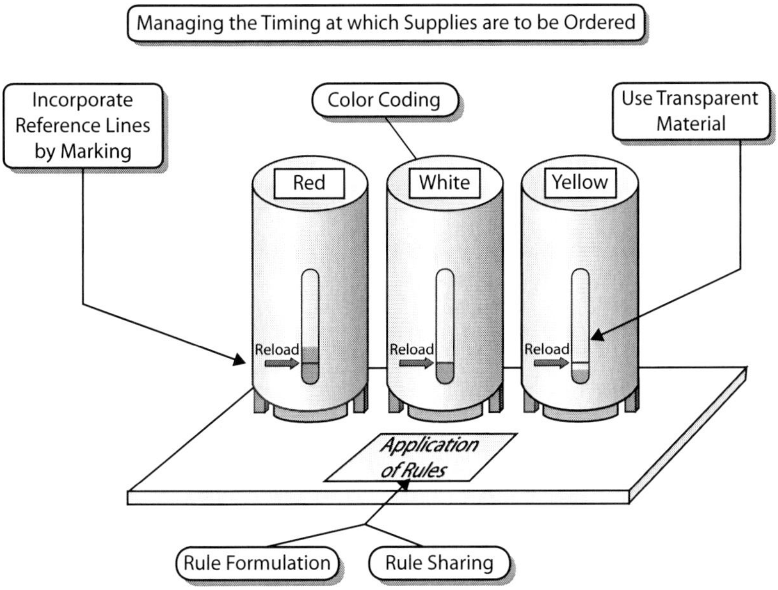

Figure 8.7 Visual Management of Supply Re-Order Point

EXAMPLE 2: MANAGING MEDICAL WARDS

Each doctor in a department is given specific colored magnets. A first board is put together with the name of the doctor and sequential numbers, along with the magnets. Then the magnets can be moved onto a management board that indicates the medical wards as well as the names of patients. This tool allows us to quickly learn which doctor is assigned to which ward and how many patients each doctor is responsible for by reading the first covered number on the board, which can be revealed by removing the magnet.

Visual Management principles used in this example are:

- Visualization — color coding
- Clarification — color coding and assigning ID numbers

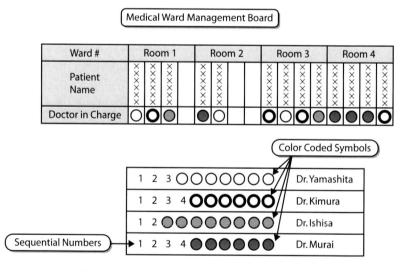

Figure 8.8 Medical Ward Management Board

EXAMPLE 3: CONTINUOUSLY IMPROVING THE WAY PATIENTS
RECEIVE DAILY MEDICATION

Patients usually take the same kinds and amount of medicine on a daily basis. Their daily intake is packaged in an individual packet that is made of transparent film so that the content of a packet can be easily identified by patients. Patients are advised to pick up an appropriate packet from a batch. Since each packet contains the same contents, patients always receive the correct dose of medicine each time.

Visual Management principles used in this example are:

- Visualization — using transparency
- Clarification — dividing medicines into one-day doses and giving a date and ID number to each packet
- Posting of rules — displaying how medicines should be taken

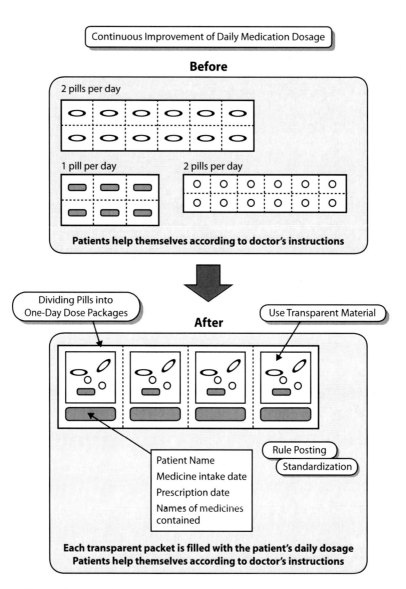

Figure 8.9 Continuous Improvement of Daily Medication Dosages

Example 4: Qualification and Technical Skills Maps

When training staff for qualifications and technical skills, a Visual Management skill map is used to express each staff member's level of certification and technical knowledge by using unique symbols, numbers, and patterns so that the it can be identified at a glance.

Visual Management principles used in this example are:

- Clarification—assigning numbers and symbols
- Sharing of rules—displaying and standardizing the level of qualifications and technical skills

Qualification and Technical Skill Maps

Standard Evaluation Ranking: Qualification Level

Level	Qualifications	Display Mode		
		Symbol	Number	Graphic
5	Ability to instruct others	S	5	●
4	Ability to complete entire job by oneself	A	4	◕
3	Ability to complete part of the job by oneself	B	3	◑
2	Ability to perform the job with assistance	C	2	◔
1	Only knowledgeable about the job	D	1	○

Standardization

Use of symbols

Use of graphs

Standard Evaluation Ranking: Technical Level

Level	Technical Ranking	Display Mode		
		Symbol	Number	Graphic
5	Ability to perform work within 80% of standardized time	S	5	●
4	Ability to perform work within standardized time	A	4	◕
3	Ability to perform work within 1.5x standardized time	B	3	◑
2	Ability to perform work within 2x standardized time	C	2	◔
1	Cannot be put in charge on his own	D	1	○

Figure 8.10 Qualification and Technical Skills Map

8-4 CASE STUDY ANALYSIS
RELATIONSHIP BETWEEN AN INCIDENT INVOLVING THE
WRONG ADMINISTRATION OF MEDICINE AND CLINICAL 5S

On February 11th, 1999 at K Hospital, Patient N, who had undergone a surgery for rheumatism the day before, was killed by receiving an I.V. of antiseptic solution that was to be used for another patient, instead of being administered an I.V. of "Heparin," a physiological saline to prevent the clotting of blood and antibiotic cells in her system. Let us analyze this incident in terms of Clinical 5S. I'd like you to consider a cause-and-effect relationship between this particular example of a medical malpractice and a utilization of Clinical 5S in the workplace.

OVERVIEW OF THE INCIDENT

Patient N, had been receiving internal medical treatment for her rheumatism problem for a period of time. After a further diagnosis, surgery became necessary to solve her problem. Her surgery did not experience any complications and she was recovering her strength very well.

At 8:25 AM on the day after the surgery, nurse A was preparing an intravenous for Patient N in the treatment room. Nurse A put an antibiotic solution of 100ml for Patient N on the medical table. The, she put a syringe containing 10ml of the Heparin Saline next to the antibiotic solution on the table. The syringe was prepared previously and stored in a refrigerator.

Next, she began preparing an intravenous for another patient. She took out a container of Chlorhexidine Gluconate solution 20% from a cabinet behind the medical table and inserted 10ml of the solution in the same type of syringe, which was then put onto the medical table for the time being. Nurse A made a memo on which she wrote with a pen, "Chlorhexidine for cleaning," and attached the label to a syringe, which was put on a tray. It is suspected that the nurse mistakenly put the memo on the syringe containing the Heparin Saline solution (Nurse A later claimed that she did not remember doing so) and put it away on a tray placed near the sink.

Around 8:30 AM, the nurse brought the antibiotic solution and a syringe to the bedside of Patient N and start administering an intravenous of antibiotic solution into the patient while leaving the syringe on the bedside. At this point, the nurse did not confirm whether or not the syringe was labeled as "Heparin Saline." The intravenous began at 8:45 AM.

Around 9:00 AM, Nurse B received a call from the patient saying that the intravenous had ended. Nurse B immediately went to the patient room to carry out the next necessary medical procedure. Nurse B picked up the syringe from a nearby tray and inserted the solution into the intravenous via the T-shaped stopcock. At this point, Nurse B also should have checked whether or not the syringe was labeled as "Heparin Saline," but she did not. It was 5 minutes before the patient began complaining about a shortage of breath and tight pain in her chest.

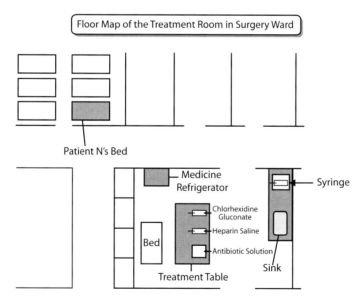

Figure 8.11 Floor Map of the Treatment Room in the Surgery Ward

ACCIDENT CAUSING FACTORS CONSIDERED BY THE MEDICAL
ACCIDENT PREVENTION STRATEGY COMMITTEE

1. Antiseptic solution, "Chlorhexidine Gluconate Solution" was prepared by using exactly the same type of syringe used for "Heparin Saline."

2. "Heparin Saline" and "Chlorhexidine Gluconate Solution" were prepared using the same medical table.

3. Label indicating "Chlorhexidine Gluconate Solution" was attached on the syringe containing "Heparin Saline."

4. The person who prepared the syringes was different from the one who administered them into the patient.

5. The syringe was kept on a small table on the bedside of the patient at all times.

6. The syringe that was put on a small table and did not get checked of its identity.

7. The actual dilution process of "Chlorhexidine Gluconate Solution" was performed in the treatment room.

ACCIDENT CAUSING FACTORS AND EFFECTIVE PREVENTATIVE STRATEGIES USING CLINICAL 5S (VISUAL MANAGEMENT)

Accident Causing Factors	Preventive Strategies	Applied Clinical 5S Concepts
Antiseptic solution, "Chlorhexidine Gluconate Solution" was prepared by using exactly the same type of syringe used for "Heparine Saline".	Clearly separate containers for medicines to be injected internally and those that are not. Color antiseptic solutions for easier identification.	Classification of containers. Color Coding.
"Heparine Saline" and "Chlorhexidine Gluconate Solution" were prepared using the same medical table.	Designate specific areas for preparation activities. Clearly mark locations where preparation should take place.	Classification of places. Marking places.
A label indicating "Chlorhexidine Gluconate Solution" was attached to the syringe containing "Heparin Saline".	Unify how syringes are to be marked. Establish specific rules. Stop using memos for identification. Place syringes in a way that the labeled side always faces up.	Unification of how information is presented. Standardization. Making rules clear. Sharing of information.
The person who prepared the syringes was different from the one who administered it into the patient.	Make it a rule to have the person who prepares the medicine administer it. If different people have to perform both preparation and administration, make clear the points to be checked and then carried out so they transition in a thorough manner.	Standardization of work and operational procedures across the organization.
The syringe was kept on a small table at the bedside of the patient at all times.	Designate specific locations for preparatory items to be placed.	
The syringe was put on a small table and did not get checked of its identity.	Make clear and share the points to be checked.	Sharing of information and checklists.
The actual dilution process of "Chlorhexidine Gluconate Solution" was performed in the treatment room.	Designate a specific location for performing dilution processes for each specific antiseptic solution.	Making clear the operational boundaries.

Table 8.1 Accident Causing Factors and Preventive Strategies

CHAPTER 9
"SUSTAIN"

9-1 IMPORTANCE OF "SUSTAIN"
WHAT IS "SUSTAIN?"

"SUSTAIN" IS ANOTHER SIGNIFICANT PRINCIPLE to implementing Clinical 5S thoroughly in a workplace. In this chapter I will describe how "Sustain" can be adapted in your organization.

"Sustain" is defined as "a process of developing a habit of complying with rules, as one should at all times." The logic behind "Sustain" is not as difficult to comprehend as we think it is. All we need to do is somehow create an organizational culture or climate in which what has to be done is routinely carried out as a habit, as if it were nothing special. Although the logic behind "Sustain" is simple and easy to understand, it is extremely challenging to adapt and maintain on an organizational level. This is because "Sustain" requires not only our understanding of the principle, but also, in order to yield positive practical results, our capacity to transform the way we think and execute appropriate actions based upon a new philosophy or ideology.

WHAT DOES IT MEAN TO "DEVELOP A HABIT"?

What is really important in this definition of "Sustain" is "developing a habit." A habit can be attained by executing a certain activity in a repetitive manner. After one becomes accustomed to performing the same task only in a certain way, one can become restless if they do not perform the activity at all or at some point will begin executing the task without even realizing it. To "develop a habit" essentially means reaching this level of mindset.

To better illustrate my point, let us analyze a common behavior of experienced car drivers. If a driver makes it a rule to always fasten the seat belt before starting the car, the driver will always extend his arm to reach for the seat belt in a subconscious state of mind.

In order to develop a habit, one must execute the same task repeatedly while following the exact same sequence of actions each time. In order to be able to repeat the same actions for a long period time, one must clearly acknowledge the meaning and objectives behind carrying out each action in a predefined way.

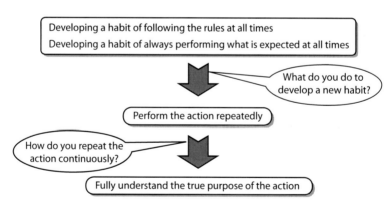

Figure 9.1 Developing a Habit

SELF-DISCIPLINE IS THE ESSENCE OF "SUSTAIN" AND THE ULTIMATE GOAL

Having been persuaded of the true meaning behind each activity, and having learned to be self-disciplined, one can act as a role model to everyone else. In order to develop a habit by continuously repeating the same tasks, one must proactively motivate oneself to do so. It is often difficult to develop a habit if one decides to repeat actions only when one is told to do so by supervisors, or when patients show up in the hospital. Instead, one has to take an independent-minded approach to initiate actions and reach a level where one can train himself by discipline from a level where he receives instructions from supervisors to behave in a certain way.

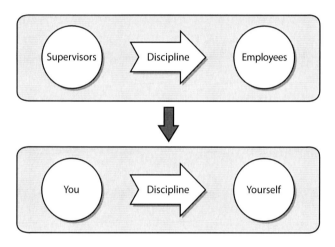

Figure 9.2 Disciplining Yourself

I understand that supervisors have to discipline their employees in the beginning stages of work so that employees can be put on the right track, however one has to go beyond that level at some point to be considered truly disciplined.

9-2 Identifying Problems Before Implementing "Sustain"

Identifying and solving problems

In order to fully realize "Sustain," supervisors have to implement it based upon the mutual understanding of employees, instead of forcing employees to follow a certain set of rules. Effective discussions have to be held with employees in which they can become persuaded of the neccessity of given instructions. Such a persuasion of employees can be achieved by following problem identification and solving processes which are specifically designed for the "Sustain" principle.

In this process of problem identification and solving for "Sustain," the important thing to do first is to make clearly understood what the ideal state is, where "Sustain" is fully realized. Supervisors should illustrate ideal working conditions with integrated "Sustain" and share the details of such a condition with their employees.

More importantly, the gap between the ideal state and the current condition has to be clearly indicated so that the current existing issues can be identified and shared with employees as a next step. Supervisors and employees should analyze, in open discussion, the reasons why the ideal state has not yet been reached or has not been able to be reached at all. This process of collectively analyzing the potential causes will eventually lead to persuading employees.

Failing to adapt "Sustain" thoroughly can be classified into 4 main causes, listed in Figure 9.5. The responsible factors are to be identified at the end of conducting careful, thorough investigations for each cause.

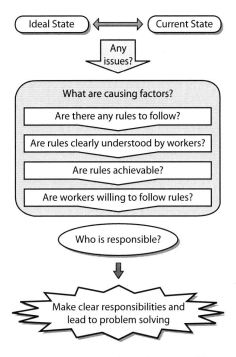

Figure 9.3 Process for Solving Problems

DEFINING THE IDEAL STATE REVEALS EXISTING PROBLEMS

Defining the ideal state requires not only some ideological explanations, but also supervisors to guide employees with practical justifications for each required activity, so that employees can understand exactly how they are expected to conduct themselves in their responsible operations. For example, in providing guidance on the ideal way for employees to report to their supervisors, employees should be advised to, "Try to make reports in a way that you are not constantly reminded to do so," instead of simply instructing them to report more often than now.

When implementing the "Sustain" concept, such an ideal state should be transformed into the "rules to be followed in a workplace" and become a part of the organizational culture. Clearly defining the ideal state with the adaptation of "Sustain" reveals how much of a gap there is between ideal and the current condition. Such a gap should be perceived as problematic and the causing factors for such a gap must be analyzed and eliminated.

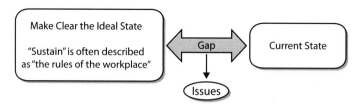

Figure 9.4 Ideal State and Existing Issues

9-3 INVESTIGATE THE CAUSE OF WORKERS' INABILITY TO FOLLOW RULES

There are certain guidelines to follow for introducing the concept of "Sustain" to your workers. For example, scolding your workers straight away can lead to an immediate backlash from them. This is not an effective method of enforcing "Sustain" in the long run, as you may realize.

So where do we start? We start by carefully analyzing why certain rules are not being followed by workers as well as the true causes for their inability to comply. Such types of cause analysis should be performed by looking at problems from 4 different perspectives (Figure 9.5), in a step-by-step manner. While taking these different perspectives into consideration we need to clearly identify what stage the essential causes for their inability originates from and redefine the responsibilities that workers need to follow for the purpose of internalizing "Sustain" into their daily operations.

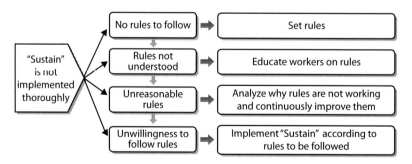

Figure 9.5 4 Steps of Cause Analysis

ARE THERE ANY RULES TO BE FOLLOWED?

The first thing to examine is whether or not the rules are clearly defined as the rules that everyone must follow. In cases where the rules are nonexistent or ambiguous, implementing "Sustain" becomes not only challenging but also results in confusion among workers. On the other hand, even if the rules are not clearly defined, there are some common rules that everyone should follow in a workplace as a minimum requirement. One such rule is to use proper manners as all humans should, such as greeting with respect and watching one's language at all times.

It is the superior's responsibility to make sure that the rules remain clearly defined at all times so that the rules don't become nonexistent or too ambiguous to follow. Unless the rules are defined and in place, "Sustain" remains a challenging principle to implement in practice. Even if the rules are clearly defined but the workers decide not to comply with those rules, the next step can be considered.

ARE THE RULES CLEARLY UNDERSTOOD BY WORKERS?

The next step is to determine if workers fully comprehend the given rules. There are many cases where workers are simply not aware of the fact that rules do exist, which of course will never lead to creating an attitude to comply with rules in the first place. For example, almost all hospitals have established some form of employment regulations that provide workers with working guidelines. However, there are many cases where some workers do not know either the exact content of such guidelines or that the guidelines exist in the first place. Needless to say, in these situations, a habit of following the organizational rules cannot be created.

On the other hand, many supervisors simply assume that their employees have already understood the commonly-used employment and organizational rules across the industry. Such supervisors will often find themselves scolding employees for not knowing certain rules. Instead, supervisors need to determine whether or not the employees have tried fulfilling their responsibility of attempting to learn about the rules. If employees did not make any actions to learn on their own, supervisors must point out that it is problematic for everyone that they did not do so.

ARE THE RULES ACHIEVABLE?

There are some cases where the rules still cannot be followed, even after the rules have been clearly identified and given the essential support and understanding from workers. Those cases are usually when certain rules become simply unachievable by any means. For example, nurse stations usually have designated locations where intravenous stands are to be placed. A problem arises when the number of intravenous stands grows to the point where the designated placement location cannot accommodate all the stands. The person in charge of managing this location is not completely free from being blamed. In this case, it does not make sense for supervisors to ask their employees to follow the rule, given that the rule is not achievable in the first place. Rather, supervisors must always perform their responsibilities for creating a work environment where rules are possible to be achieved at any given time.

On the other hand, employees are also responsible for reporting to their supervisors in order to keep them updated on the current working situations. If certain rules become unachievable, the situation needs to be reported by contacting the supervisors about the issues to be discussed, in order to draw out effective solutions. Supervisors need to make sure that their employees are capable of contacting supervisors, reporting, and discussing the problems as well.

UNWILLINGNESS TO FOLLOW THE RULES

There is a fundamental difference between the facts, "workers cannot achieve the rules" and "workers will not achieve the rules." In the former case, supervisors who give instructions to employees are primarily responsible for ensuring that the rules can be met. However, we still encounter some workers who are unwilling to comply with the rules even when everything else is in place.

How can supervisors change the attitudes of these people? This can be done by reviewing each phase of rule-setting, as I have described in this chapter thus far, and clearly redefining the responsibilities that must be fulfilled by those who are unwilling, as well as the responsibilities of the supervisors. Supervisors should provide them, or sometimes scold them if needed, with specific instructions and continuous improvement ideas so that they will learn to follow the rules. Scolding is effective only when the targeted person understands the reason why they are being treated a certain way and have a clear understanding of the responsibilities that they must fulfill.

I cannot stress enough that defining responsibilities for each key player is extremely crucial in implementing "Sustain," so that the rules are always followed across the organization. Both the instructor and instructed must acknowledge their responsibilities and be committed to fulfilling their duties in the process. Clearly defining responsibilities across the organization will lead to effective methods for the implementation of "Sustain," which each staff member can agree upon in a collective manner.

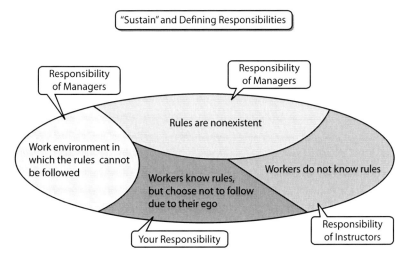

Figure 9.6 "Sustain" and Defining Responsibilities

9-4 HOW TO MAINTAIN THE CONTINUITY OF CLINICAL 5S

Maintaining the continuity of Clinical 5S activities is another significant challenge for us to overcome. It is manageable for many hospitals to yield positive results by adapting Clinical 5S over a short period of time, such as 1-2 years. However, it often requires hospitals to devote a tremendous level of resources and energy in order to maintain continuous Clinical 5S implementation and benefit from the desirable results over a much longer period of time.

What makes it so difficult to maintain the continuity of Clinical 5S? The biggest reason is the fact that the positive attitudes among top executives and members of an implementation committee toward Clinical 5S have a tendency to diminish over time. Workers are extremely sensitive to this type of change in upper management and their diminished attitudes, as well as the lack of positivity, will soon disperse across the organization, resulting in a stagnant state of implementation activities and efforts.

On the other hand, the level of Clinical 5S competency of the organization is also likely to decline when the staff begins feeling overly satisfied with current results. To solve this, a mindset that continues to inspire everyone to set higher standards needs to be nurtured in every single staff member.

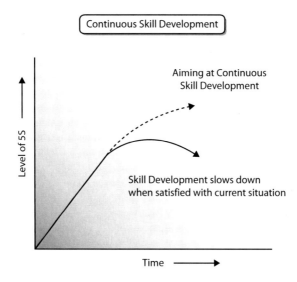

Figure 9.7 Continuous Skill Development

How to Avoid Becoming Satisfied with the Current Situation

In order to prevent workers from becoming overly content with the current results, a mechanism is needed that motivates workers to want the current Clinical 5S practices to evolve to a higher level. The following points are the guidelines for establishing such a mechanism in the organization.

1. Set higher objectives.

   Setting objectives for Clinical 5S should be integrated into the process of establishing corporate management policies at the beginning of each year. Develop a habit of setting higher standards intentionally and nurture a challenging mentality to achieve goals.

2. Modify the content of checklists.

   Using the same checklists repeatedly makes staff members feel as if they are stuck in a rut, especially those who feel over-confident with themselves by having always scored the highest evaluation points. Therefore it is important to modify checklists on a regular basis so that workers always feel challenged.

3. Assign supervisory roles to a wide range of people.

   It is true that one's level of being able to competently and accurately assessing Clinical 5S will greatly improve as one continues to evaluate many other workplaces. Therefore a wide range of workers, besides managers and members of implementation committees, should receive supervisory responsibilities in one way or another.

4. Clinical 5S for work is the ultimate goal.

   Another effective way of preventing workers from becoming satisfied with the current condition is to require them to apply the Clinical 5S concepts not only to items but also to the content of their own work. In other words, workers can learn to implement "Sort" and "Set in Order" concepts to their work responsibilities in order to achieve a higher level of efficiency.

Maintain continuous improvement efforts

Continuous improvement efforts have to be maintained in order to improve the quality of Clinical 5S and avoid becoming satisfied with current results. The targets of continuous improvement also have to be changed. It is important for all of us to recognize that a workplace keeps transforming itself as long as we keep seeking desirable results by our continuous improvement efforts, in a persistent manner. A mindset that seeks to maintain the current situation and insufficient commitment to ensuring the thoroughness of implementation will assist us only in failing when trying to sustain effective Clinical 5S implementation over time.

REASONS WHY THE THOROUGHNESS OF CLINICAL 5S IMPLEMENTATION IS NECESSARY

Implementing Clinical 5S in a thorough manner means that Clinical 5S activities are embedded into our daily activities. This can never be true if you took even a single half measure toward adapting Clinical 5S. Human beings have a strong desire to maintain cleanliness in a place they have tried so hard to make clean, however a dirty area can easily spread if nothing is done to it. To put this into perspective, if you mix a rotten orange in with a box of other oranges, all of the oranges will become rotten much faster. The same thing can happen in terms of Clinical 5S. In other words, if there is even a single dirty place left after having adapted Clinical 5S to a certain degree, that dirty place will put everything out of balance. Therefore it is extremely critical to implement Clinical 5S in an absolute manner with careful attention to every detail.

WHAT DOES IT MEAN TO IMPLEMENT CLINICAL 5S IN A "THOROUGH" MANNER?

A thorough manner means a condition where Clinical 5S is adapted in every nook and corner, leaving no unfinished places, with attention to detail. The following are areas that remain challenging to do just that:

- "Sorting" inside storage units
- "Standardizing" how wheelchairs and carts for transporting medical appliances are used
- "Set in Order" the highest and lowest shelf of a cabinet or storage shelves
- "Sorting" and "Setting in Order" inside drawers
- "Shining" the corners of floors
- "Shining" laundry rooms and waste disposal rooms
- "Shining" under the beds

Now, let us look at what ought to be done, in terms of our mindset and know-how, to ensure a thorough implementation of Clinical 5S.

SHARE THE IDEAL STATE OF CLINICAL 5S IMPLEMENTATION

The first thing to do is to convey to workers what the ideal state of Clinical 5S should look like in their workplace. Sharing such expectations is extremely important and is the key to a successful implementation. Effective methods of sharing such critical information are either having the members of implementation committees go audit workplaces or inviting external consultants for their expert instructions on the matter. The main purpose of this strategy is to allow workers to realize the real problems by analyzing the reasons why certain aspects of their implementation approach were criticized.

It is true to say that staff in hospitals that are at a premature stage of Clinical 5S implementation generally fail to recognize a unified goal for what the ideal state of their organization should look like, and often suffer from differences in opinion toward the expected level of implementation thoroughness that ought to be accomplished. This is also true of organizations and workplaces that are struggling to adapt Clinical 5S in a thorough manner, even though they have spent more resources in their attempt. This type of a lack of uniformity remains a serious obstacle in implementing Clinical 5S in an absolute manner.

TOUR OTHER WORKPLACES WITH A HIGH LEVEL OF ACHIEVEMENT IN CLINICAL 5S IMPLEMENTATION

In order to demonstrate to workers what you mean by the ideal state of Clinical 5S implementation, take them to other accomplished workplaces so that they can observe with their own eyes. After all, a picture is worth a thousand words.

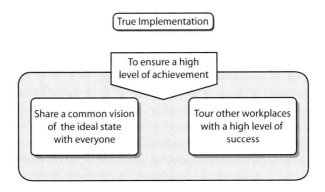

Figure 9.8 True 5S Implementation

CHAPTER 10

THE FUTURE OF CLINICAL 5S AT TAKEDA GENERAL HOSPITAL

10-1 CHALLENGES OF TAKEDA GENERAL HOSPITAL

TAKEDA GENERAL HOSPITAL PROVIDES 1,097 patient rooms and is located in Wakamatsu City in the Aizu region (population of 320,000) of Fukushima Prefecture (population of 2,100,000 as of August, 2004), Japan. Wakamatsu City has 15% of the prefectural population, while taking up approximately 40% of the entire prefectural area.

24.5% of the population of the Aizu region consists of elderly citizens who are above the age of 65, which is relatively high compared to other cities. There are two other large hospitals in Wakamatsu City that provide more than 500 patient rooms each. According to a report conducted by prefectural official on the existing allocation of medical care, the Aizu medical district is offering about 2,000 wards (rooms), which is considered to be excessive for the demand for rooms, which is around 1,000.

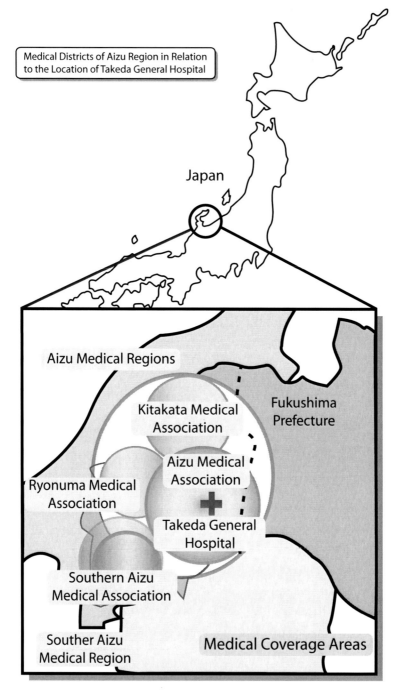

Figure 10.1 Map of Medical Districts relative to Takeda General Hospital

Various changes in the social condition, such as lower birth rates, an aging population, and bubble recessions, have negatively impacted local medical communities, which can no longer stay in business unless they change the way they operate. Hospitals have to take into consideration the unique trend among the general population in which patients have begun to be much more specific about their expectations for their treatments and the medical safety that is to be provided by hospitals. Patients are also starting to choose a certain hospital, as they have various resources to research in advance the competency level of a hospital's doctors and staff and many statistical records which indicate the number of successful surgeries and treatments in the past. Even when patients do not see any difference in such aspects I feel that patients have much stronger expectations than they have had in the past for desiring a higher level of quality and comfort from whichever hospital they end up choosing.

Principle	Meaning
Sort (Seiri)	Classify into necessary items and unnecessary items and dispose of unnecessary items
Set in Order (Seiton)	Designate how and where items are placed so that necessary items can be obtained easily
Shine (Seiso)	Maintain immaculate environment by cleaning and performing inspections
Standardize (Seiketsu)	Develop a habit so that rules are followed properly at all times
Sustain (Shitsuke)	Execute "Sort", "Set in Order", and "Shine" in a thorough manner and maintain cleanliness

Figure 10.2 Meaning of each "S" in 5S

In these circumstances, it has become extremely important for hospitals to establish an organizational mechanism that allows them to meet the expectations of patients in both timely and precise manners. Given the fact that hospitals are essentially collective entities that consist of the specialized expertise of medical professionals, each individual's proficiency in being able to execute their duties is an indispensable asset to the hospital. Therefore, hospitals have been able to provide the public with the highest quality of medical care because they are supported by such remarkable people within the industry.

However, as various societal situations keep changing, hospitals have ceased depending upon only the unique capacity of each medical professional and begun working toward achieving techniques that are designed to ensure they are providing the best and safest services to patients. This is achieved by creating a mechanism in which every single medical staff member is able to perform any necessary operation in an efficient manner by eliminating Miri (unreasonable work), Muda (wastes) and Mura (unevenness of work).

Many innovative systems that are now utilized in hospitals, such as integrated healthcare, clinical pathway, electronic medical charts, management objectives, SPD (Supply Processing & Distribution), and cost management, are the by-products of new strategies to accommodate such various changes.

However, the principle issues that the staff faced prior to the implementation of Clinical 5S were important enough that they felt something had to be done about, at the fundamental level, before proper implementation could occur. Staff suffered from Miri (unreasonable work), Muda (wastes), and Mura (unevenness of work) of inefficient operations, which were generated from simple problems such as dealing with missing medical supplies during a shift change, keeping track of borrowed equipment among departments without an automated system, and so on.

10-2 WHY CLINICAL 5S WAS CHOSEN

Takeda General Hospital strongly believes that a hospital is allowed to exist as an organization by earning substantial trust and satisfaction from the community by intertwining the gift of each medical professional with larger organizational structures, and that a hospital must continue transforming itself in order to seek the next level of contribution to the public. With this fundamental philosophy in mind, their team searched for the most effective method for conveying these obligations to staff members.

In 2000, the hospital implemented the Management by Objective (MBO) as its leading strategy to put the hospital on the right track. MBO was a breakthrough mechanism that allowed each staff member to set their own objectives and plans of action. Consequently, the overall financial results and operational efficiency of the hospital improved. As a result of each staff member having accomplished their objectives, they received incentives of financial benefits in return. MBO also eliminated the traditional bureaucratic mindset of "whoever inhibits change wins."

After MBO was put in place, the staff hardly complained that upper management failed to keep them updated about new directions that they wanted to take the hospital in. The hospital staff was much more excited about making the objectives come true for what mattered to them the most at the time. However, as organizational objectives were announced and became the main focus of the hospital's daily resources, a tendency to postpone the problem solving effort of each staff member's objectives was unavoidable in the workplace. As a result, the team, along with the involvement staff at the actual place of work, began once again looking for something that could allow them to seek tangible results on a workplace level.

Around this time they happened to learn about an electronic manufacturing company called Iwaki Electronics, whose factory was successful in increasing its productivity by implementing 5S. They became extremely interested in discovering what this company did, exactly. It was around the end of 2000, as I remember.

Having a deep history of establishment, Takeda General Hospital at the time was suffering from aging building structures and outdated medical equipment, as well as an accumulation of unnecessary items on the floors. At the same time, the hospital's urgency to install cutting-edge medical devices was quite prominent, which resulted in a lack of sufficient working space.

Therefore establishing an efficient and safe working environment was the first priority that the hospital had to focus on. Even though the 5S concept, "Sort," "Set in Order," "Shine," "Standardize," and "Sustain" did not have the same level of excitement and brilliance that new medical equipment entertained them with, they acknowledged that 5S had a mechanism built in for allowing every single staff member to identify the most critical issues associated with each workplace and formulate solutions through having discussions and executing strategies.

When the team from the hospital toured the shop floors of the Iwaki Electronics factory they received valuable explanations from the supervisors about their remarkable continuous improvements, such as improving the quality of each process by adapting 5S, a Kaizen suggestion system among workers, coordinating with suppliers, reducing wastes, becoming environmentally sustainable, and more. These concepts were clearly apparent to all of them and turned their thinking completely around, as they had always wanted to implement only a better method of communication among their workers based upon certain commonly used slogans. It was long after this experience in touring the shop floor when they learned that many of their own team members had discovered what they were really looking for in terms of the most effective way of yielding efficiency in hospital operations.

As I have described thus far, 5S activities are the minimum requirement for any organization. 5S builds a solid foundation for achieving such purposes as gaining a higher level of operating efficiency, eliminating human errors and medical accidents, and attaining an optimal use of available working space through utilizing "Sort," "Set in Order," "Shine," "Standardize," and "Sustain" principles for items, information, and human resources. The term "minimum requirement" can be viewed as common-sense behaviors to be carried out by workers on a daily basis, however such common-sense behaviors are extremely challenging to instill among workers. For example, such fundamental operational rules as greeting each other in a respectful manner, putting items back where they belong, being habitually punctual, and keeping promises requires a synchronization of the behaviors of every single staff member, which will eventually progress into transforming the entire organizational culture within a company.

Since their experience on the factory shop floor they had begun to carefully analyze how to establish a mechanism in their own daily work which could allow them to fully draw out the underlying talents and creativity of their strongest weapon — 1,600 employees. However, they also felt that it would be extremely challenging and require a tremendous amount of their resources and commitment to catch up to the level of accomplishment acquired by Iwaki Electronics.

10-3 EXECUTING IMPLEMENTATION

In April of 2001, the 5S implementation committee was created with Dr. Kobato (currently the assistant director of Takeda General Hospital) as the chairman. They began by establishing: 1) the intent of Clinical 5S implementation, 2) objectives, and 3) implementation phases, as well as rough guidelines for identifying appropriate execution periods for each of the different 5S principles. The team also decided to actively obtain external help from expert 5S consultants, in order to operate at a higher level of proficiency as an organization in an objective manner. So the hospital invited me into their organization, since I had successfully transformed Iwaki Electronics to what it is today, as the main instructor for Clinical 5S implementation.

IMPLEMENTATION EXECUTION OBJECTIVES

1. Intent of Clinical 5S implementation.

   A medium-term structural reform (3 – 5 year planning) that is aimed at organizational quality, safety, and productivity.

2. Objectives of Clinical 5S activities.

   The followings are the objectives targeted toward increasing quality, safety, and productivity:

   - *Management standards*

     Increase the level of management standards for items and time allocation.

   - *Increasing the quality and dignity of the hospital and its staff*

     Recognize the true value of every item and work time in order to become a hospital and staff with the highest level of quality and dignity possible.

   - *Building an energized organizational culture*

     Achieving the 2 first objectives will transform the stagnant organizational functions into energized functions within the organization.

3. Implementation phases.

Planned 5S implementation stages are as follows:

Dates	Implementation Stage
May - June, 2001	Enhancing the awareness of 5S
May - June, 2001	Workshops and formulation of strategies (Theme:"Sort" and "Set in Order")
June, 2001 - February, 2002	Execution of "Sort" and "Set in Order"
April - May, 2002	Follow-up education/training for "Sort" and "Set in Order"
May - June, 2002	Workshops and formulation of strategies (Theme:"Shine","Standardize", and "Sustain")
May, 2002 - February, 2003	Execution of "Shine","Standardize", and "Sustain"
March, 2003	Execute continuous improvement ideas based on the overall evaluation of 5S achievement
April, 2003 - March, 2004	Continue to perform implementation strategies and frequent diagnostics of up-to-date results

Table 10.1 Planned Implementation Stages Calendar

CHAPTER 11
EXECUTING CLINICAL 5S ACTIVITIES

11-1 THE MASTER PLAN

THE ORIGINAL 5S IMPLEMENTATION MEMBERS of Takeda General Hospital initialized their Clinical 5S activities by bringing the organization together and educating managers. Several section manager-class executive members and ten 5S implementation leaders were selected to be fully trained on the fundamental principles of 5S, as well as practical implementation methodologies. On top of that, they assigned 5S execution leaders (about 100 leaders at the time—it is currently about 160) from each work place and planned four intensive training workshops, as well as frequent study missions to the factories operated by Iwaki Electronics.

They decided that all of the 5S implementation activities were to be carried out in groups with a specific execution leader assigned. Therefore, in order to promise the most practical content for training, they asked me to be their main instructor. Concurrently, they began rearranging their warehouse space in order to store various unnecessary items that were collected from different workplaces through having practiced the very first stage of 5S, "Sort," exclusively. As a result, the quantity of items that had been left alone due to their unclear purposes was able to fill up 2 large containers. Based on this activity, supported by the kick-off announcement made by the chairman of the committee, Mr. Kobato, the entire hospital continued implementing 5S for about 6 months.

Consequently, 5S activities were welcomed into every single work place in the hospital much more intensely than what the implementation committee had expected. Mr. Kobato had this to say about the unexpected enthusiasm, "We wish that we could say that this positive reaction was due to the master plan we had created, however it was clearly because of Mr. Takahara, who had conducted a thorough preliminary evaluation and analysis of our work environment."

When I stepped into their workplaces to conduct inspections for the very first time, the staff showed a resistance by saying, "Do not open drawers without asking first," "Do not wander around taking photos of random things," and so on. The staff did not believe that I could understand that there are huge differences between situations in a hospital and those in an ordinary company and tried to discredit me. However, they are currently appreciating the results and are now willing to share their improved workplace with anyone who is interested.

It is impossible to prove with any quantitative analysis at this point that accidents are more likely to occur in areas where we do not desire other people to visit, and keeping these places unexposed would simply fail to address the real issues at hand. The hospital had recently learned, in a hard way, that creating opportunities for other people to come and analyze their workplace is the most effective way of preventing accidents from occurring, and frequent audits of 5S progress are the ideal tool to provide us with such opportunities.

For the first round of audits I conducted, 120 different workplaces were checked from 9AM to 5PM without taking any solid breaks. Each workplace was scored and documented by photographs, while encouraging the staff to participate in close discussions to address specific issues at hand. Figure 11.1 describes the results of such audits.

Rank	Workplace	5S Leader	Implementation Leader	Score	Evaluation Grade
1	OT Room	∞ ∞	∞ ∞	75	A
2	Nutrition Division	∞ ∞	∞ ∞	74	A
3	Warehouse	∞ ∞	∞ ∞	73	A
4	ICU	∞ ∞	∞ ∞	72	A
5	Prescription Laboratory	∞ ∞	∞ ∞	71	A
5	Medical Admin. Division #2 General Affair Section	∞ ∞	∞ ∞	71	A
7	Medical Examination Information Division	∞ ∞	∞ ∞	70	A
8	Ashinomaki Onsen Hospital Rehabilitation OT	∞ ∞	∞ ∞	69	B
9	Ashinomaki Onsen Hospital Rehabilitation ST	∞ ∞	∞ ∞	68	B
10	Pathological Laboratory	∞ ∞	∞ ∞	67	B
10	Urology Department	∞ ∞	∞ ∞	67	B
10	DI Laboratory	∞ ∞	∞ ∞	67	B
13	Home Nursery Care Support Ofc.	∞ ∞	∞ ∞	66	B
13	Physical Check-up Center Administration Office	∞ ∞	∞ ∞	66	B
15	DM Center	∞ ∞	∞ ∞	65	B
15	Pharmaceutical Laboratory	∞ ∞	∞ ∞	65	B
17	Medical Admin. Division #1 / Outpatient Reception Section	∞ ∞	∞ ∞	64	B
17	Medical Admin. Division #1 / Outpatient Section	∞ ∞	∞ ∞	64	B
17	Eminence 2F	∞ ∞	∞ ∞	64	B
20	Main Chief Nurse Office	∞ ∞	∞ ∞	63	B
21	Medical Admin. #2 Division / Patient Acceptance Division	∞ ∞	∞ ∞	62	B
21	Medical Admin. #1 Division / Outpatient Management Division	∞ ∞	∞ ∞	62	B
23	South Building #2 - 2F	∞ ∞	∞ ∞	61	B
23	Admin. Division of Psychiatric Dept.	∞ ∞	∞ ∞	61	B
25	Internal Medicine Department	∞ ∞	∞ ∞	60	B
25	Gastral Department	∞ ∞	∞ ∞	60	B
25	Admin. Division / Day-Care Center	∞ ∞	∞ ∞	60	B
25	Management Planning Division	∞ ∞	∞ ∞	60	B
29	Day-Care Center for Psychiatric Dept.	∞ ∞	∞ ∞	58	C
29	Hospital Administration Division / Human Resources	∞ ∞	∞ ∞	58	C

Figure 11.1 Evaluation of 120 Workplaces

Surprisingly, it is believed that it is the uniquely competitive characteristic of the medical professionals that hospitals employ that often inspire them to do things better than their colleagues can in other workplaces. Their staff has retained a positive attitude for continuing to do their best at producing positive 5S results, which they believe is the main cause for having exceeded our initial expectations.

We are extremely proud of the staff and were impressed by receiving a positive comment from Mr. Ryutaro Kono, a Special Researcher at Tepco Electric Power Co., when he came to the hospital to conduct a workshop on the prevention of medical malpractices. He said "Every staff member in the hospital appears extremely lively and motivated to practice 5S, as if they are playing a fun game with one another."

11-2 ACTUAL IMPLEMENTATION PROCEDURES

The following figures (Figures 11.2, 11.3, and 11.4) are the actual documents that were used for initializing the 5S implementation in Takeda General Hospital.

Participation Request Letter

April 10, 2001

Kobato Medical Examination Section Chief

We have made a decision to initiate Clinical 5S implementation starting this year. I would like to kindly ask your participation in the newly-formed implementation team, also known as the "Brain Team."

As for 5S training for our general staff, responsible managers and 5S leaders will be in charge of conducting various workshops that follow the sequence of "Sort," "Set in Order," "Shine," "Standardize," and "Sustain" principles.

However, in order to avoid a passive training curriculum for our stuff, the Brain Team is obligated to establish a solid foundation for 5S implementation and act as the leading role in executing the 5S adaptation strategies across the organization.

For details about our first meeting, please refer to the information below:

Name of the Meeting:
The First 5S Strategy Meeting with the Brain Team

Date / Time: Location:
15:00- 17:00 - Thur., April, 12, 2001   Meeting Room 10 F

Expert Implementor:
Akio Takahara from Basic Management Laboratory

Team Members:

Kobato Medical Examination Section Leader ● Kanome General Manager
Suzuki Operational Dept. Section Manager ● Suzuki Chief Nurse
Hasegawa Rehabilitation Chief Technician ● Suzuki Operational Management
Ohta Nursing Care Dept. Section Manager
Azuse Business Management Dept. Section Manager

- President Takanao Aoki
Takeda General Hospital

Figure 11.2 Participation Request Letter

To Affiliated Departments

Business Administration Department

Under the announcement of our president, we have decided to implement Clinical 5S across the hospital. Goals of our 5S implementation consist of 4 primary points, described below.

1. Aim to achieve a hospital work environment where 5S is thoroughly implemented.
2. Improve the management skills of respective managers through 5S activities.
3. Realize ideal working condition through implementing 5S.
4. Establish a working environment where medical accidents can always be prevented thorough implementing 5S.

Instructor Takahara is planning on visiting our work areas and conducting an assessment on his own. We have not been informed of where he will be visiting as it will be decided by Takahara when he arrives in the hospital. In case he chooses to visit your workplace, kindly show him around and answer any questions that he may have. Thank you very much for your attention.

Overview:

● Instructor: Akio Takahara from Basic Management Laboratory
● Visit Date/Time: Thursday, April, 12, 2001   9:00-15:00
● Location: To be determined by Takahara instructor on the visiting day

What is 5S?

"Sort" - Seiri	Dispose of unnecessary items
"Set in Order" Sciton	Create a work environment where necessary items can be immediately retrieved for use
"Shine" - Seisou	Clean your work area by removing waste
"Standardize" - Seiketsu	Maintain cleanliness in your work area
"Sustain" - Shitsuke	Develop a habit of following common rules at all times

Figure 11.3 Clinical 5S Implementation Introductory Letter

5S Implementation Action Plan Ideas
(Including feedback and approvals from the 5S Committee)

1. Main Purpose of 5S implementation
   Transform the organization to one with a higher level of quality, safety, and productivity over 3-5 year time frame.

2. Goals of 5S activities
   The following goals will be met for improving the quality of our services, safety, and productivity.
   (1) Improving management standards for items and work time
   (2) Improving the quality of services and the dignity of our hospital as a whole to become a worker or hospital with a high degree of quality and dignity by acknowledging the true value of items and work time as well as improving management standards
   (3) Revitalizing the organizational culture - an organization can transform itself into an energized entity by realizing the goals described above

3. Implementation period of 5S activities (Goal: May, 2001 - March, 2004)
   (1) Preparation period (May - June, 2001)
   (2) Implementation execution period (June, 2001 - March, 2003)
   (3) Follow-up period (April, 2003 - March, 2004)

4. Content of implementation
   (1) Basic Guidelines
   ① Conduct workshops targeted towards management level workers and promote continuous improvement on a work area basis
   ② Obtain assistance from external expert consultants
   ③ Implement across existing organizations under the foundation

   (2) 5S Implementation Schedules
   ① May - June, 2001: 5S vision uplifting
   ② May - June, 2001: Workshops and action planning
   (Target "Sort" and "Set in Order")
   ③ June, 2001 - Feburary, 2002: Implement "Sort" and "Set in Order"
   ④ March, 2002: Execute continuous improvement based on assessment thus far
   ⑤ April - May, 2002: Follow-up training on "Sort" and "Set in Order"
   ⑥ May - June, 2002: Workshops and action planning
   (Target "Shine," "Standardize," and "Sustain")
   ⑦ May, 2002 - Feburary, 2003: Implement "Shine," "Standardize," and "Sustain"
   ⑧ March, 2003: Execute continuous improvement based on assessment thus far
   ⑨ April - March, 2003: Execute "Sustain" strategies and maintain a regular analysis of sustainment level

Figure 11.4.1 5S Implementation Action Plan Letter

5. Upcoming events
   (1) Planned workshops
   ① For 5S leaders: May 22 and 23
   ② For implementation leaders: 2-day training scheduled to tale place in June
   (2) The Brain Team meeting schedule
   ① Two meetings planned for May (May 14th and 28th)
   ② The team to create a list of items to be considered
   ③ The team to create "To Do Lists"
   (3) Execute a large-scale cleaning across the organization in addition to implemented "Shine" chores in each work area.
6. Implementation Framework
   (1) Implementation Headquarter
   ① Slogan - "Let's create a friendly workplace by 5S!" etc.
   (2) Implementation framework
   5S Implementation Headquarters
   Implementation Committee Meeting (Brain Team meeting)
   Each workplace
   Chief Director - President
   Committee Chairman - Kobato Medical Examination Section Leader

Prep	Training (Manager/Leaders) - Workplace inspection (finalizing target areas) - Work area debriefing and formulating action plans customized for each work area
"Sort"	Create "Sort" action plan - Photographing "Before" photos - Execute "Sort" - Eliminate unnecessary items (Red tagging)
"Set in Order"	Create "Set in Order" action plan - Assign action groups - Formulate action plan per group
"Shine"	Conduct a workplace-based assessment of "Shine" implementation - Reconfirm "Shine" rules - Conduct 5S Audits specific to each workplace
"Standardize"	Photographing "After" shots - Comparison between "Before" and "After" documentation and presentation of results
"Sustain"	Finalizing "Shine" targeted areas - Establish "Shine" rules for each workplace - Execute "Shine"

Items to consider for future implementation:
① Necessary supplies
② Budget
③ Appropriate spending allowance for each work place
④ Selection of implementation leaders
⑤ Implementation strategy map (including decisions from each workplace)
Make clear each responsibilities of each workplace
⑥ Methods of monitoring implementation progress
⑦ Checking consistency with nursing responsibilities

Submit your plans to instructor Takahara and receive his feedback on each item.

Figure 11.4.2 5S Implementation Action Plan Letter

CHAPTER 12

CLINICAL 5S ACTIVITIES THAT ARE PRACTICED AT THE ACTUAL PLACE OF WORK

12-1 CASE STUDY: INTERNAL MEDICINE NURSING DEPARTMENT

12-1-1 CONDITION AND ISSUES PRIOR TO 5S IMPLEMENTATION

BEFORE 5S IMPLEMENTATION, THE WORKPLACE was basically a chaos of items that were placed all over tables in order to simply allow easier access for every worker. Items were not labeled and looking for specific items was extremely challenging for everyone. Medical supplies were also overstocked at all times so that they did not have to be filled as frequently, and the staff felt much more comfortable knowing that items would not run out when they were needed.

12-1-2 ACTIVITY PROGRESS

1. Progress achieved in the first year.

Even though the "Kick-off" declaration was made, the whole process started without people having gained a full comprehension of the activities to be executed. Managers were able to assign responsibilities to each dedicated staff person, however, managers themselves failed to sufficiently allocate their own time for practicing 5S activities, as their busy work schedules could not be sacrificed. Also, the guidelines that were supposed to help staff in determining which items ought to be disposed of were not clear enough throughout the organization, which prevented the staff from performing "Sort" and assigning clear identification to each item in a timely manner. In such undesirable conditions, 5S activities were limited to the efforts of managers and implementation leaders, while failing to ensure the full support from the entire staff.

2. Progress achieved in the second year.

In an attempt to make up for the low-performing results from the 1st year, we rolled our sleeves up again after having redefined the responsibilities for each team at the actual place of work. Despite all that, we still faced a condition where the very limited workplaces were filled with a variety of items. In order to create sufficient space to be used communally, the drawers used by nurses were moved to the break room as a preliminary part of our "Sort" activities. This allowed us to label places for certain items to be stored in. However, the situation where managers and 5S implementation leaders were the only dedicated participants still remained the same in the second year.

3. Progress achieved in the third year.

For the reason that placement locations of items and how items should be stored were not yet identified comprehensively, we were not able to dispel the complicated perspectives that our staff had toward implementing Clinical 5S. Therefore, we decided to start over by carefully revisiting "Sort" principles.

We realized that we did not do a good job cultivating an accurate awareness toward Clinical 5S among our staff initially. Our 5S implementation leaders began close discussions to review the common rules established for executing "Sort" and "Set in Order." 5S implementation leaders worked closely with responsible staff for managing 5S while focusing on the following rules:

- Consolidate items that are of similar characteristics
- Make a better use of recycled materials
- Color code items based on identifications and uses
- Enforce labeling of items

By asking our staff to implement these rules we began gaining positive support from them in striving for positive results. Some of the positive results were, for example, the need for handwriting on a white board being eliminated by adapting the use of magnets, and items being placed in designated locations with clear identification labels. We also asked each of the managers of 5S activities in each area of work to declare a constant quantity of items to be placed within each placement location. As a result the number of items in each workplace were decreased and, since every item was placed in a certain way, it significantly altered how organized workplaces appeared in everyone's eye. However, this type of activity was still centered on certain personnel and full participation from the entire staff remained a challenge for the future.

4. Progress achieved in the forth year.

Having reflected upon our course of action for the first 3 years, we set a new goal for the 4th year, which was committed to achieving the full-fledged participation of every single staff member in 5S implementation, as well as eliminating any activities carried out by limited personnel. In other words, we transformed the 5S activities into organization-wide objectives to be carefully administered by each responsible hospital ward.

Given that this year's primary plan of action was "Shine," once again we began by enhancing the motivation of staff members toward implementing 5S. The staff was divided into groups so that the responsibilities of each key player, such as managers, 5S implementation leaders, and 5S managing supervisors, would to be clearly indicated.

As for the specific content of our 5S activities during this year, the staff was segregated into 5 different groups, with the 5S implementation leaders becoming group leaders in order to monitor and instruct the progress that each team made. Then, study groups were arranged to cover the fundamentals of 5S activities in the hope of inspiring the staff and increasing their awareness toward 5S. Each 5S managing supervisor also carefully analyzed the ideal state of the workplace he was in charge of and was asked to submit a plan proposal document describing his unique strategies for adapting 5S, including "Shine." In doing so, we asked 5S managing supervisors to make sure that the opinions of the team members, not only in his team but also in other teams, were incorporated into the plan of action. 5S implementation leaders performed a regulatory role to oversee this process.

Designating routine inspection dates enabled us to implement 5S as planned, gradually and surely. The goal was to carry out such inspections 3 times a month by utilizing the monthly inspection checklist form, described in Figure 12.2.

5S Targeted Areas and Responsibility Sharing

	Group Leader	Managing Supervisor	Target Area
1G			
2G			
3G			
4G			
5G			

Figure 12.1 5S Targeted Areas and Responsibility Sharing

| Evaluation Form for "Sort" and Supply Management |

★ Enter score between 0-5 according to the 5S evaluation standards

Target Area			Primarily Evaluation	Intermediate Evaluation	Final Evaluation
Managing Supervisor			Self	Leader	Managing Supervisor
	No.	Checklist			
"Sort"	1	There are no unnecessary items around target areas or on surrounding floors			
	2	There are no unnecessary items within target areas			
	3	There are an appropriate amount of items, not exceeding what is really needed			
	4	"Sort" activities are carried out on a regular basis			
3 Elements of "Set in Order"	5	Designated placement area for each item is clearly identified			
	6	Designated placement area for each item is clearly labeled			
	7	Designated placement area for each item is clearly classified			
	8	Items are not placed outside of boundaries			
	9	Designated placement area for each item and the 5S Managing Supervisors name are clearly displayed			
	10	Labels and marking tapes are still intact; without tears and wear			
	11	Items are placed in accurate locations and match with labels			
	12	Items are placed in either a parallel or perpendicular manner			
Visual Management	13	Visual management is maintained throughout			
	14	Appropriate fixed quantity of each item is clearly identified			
	15	Replenishment point for each item is clearly displayed			
	16	Color coding is effectively utilized			
Implementation Procedures	17	Every member of the team is always following the "Set in Order" rules			
	18	Full participation towards 5S implementation is maintained			
	19	Each team member is proactively sharing improvement ideas for overall 5S success			
	20	"Set in Order" action plan is well-established and progress is being made to meet expectations			
		Total			

Figure 12.2 Evaluation Form for "Sort" and Supply Management

Frequent inspections were carried out in the order of 5S managing supervisor, group leader, then manager. Evaluating a workplace in this manner enabled the staff to clearly learn "By When?," "Where?," and "How?" for each scheduled 5S activity and effectively propose meaningful objectives for the following month.

Visual Management was also in place at all times by utilizing white boards, filing cabinets, and various other storage cabinets for files and medicines, and as such were labeled with constant quantities so that the point which prompts orders for restocking or purchasing of necessary items was made clear. The biggest achievement of this year was being able to see frequent discussions among the staff exchanging ideas for improving 5S implementation, through which their full participation was ensured.

12-1-3 LESSONS LEARNED FROM THE IMPLEMENTATION PROCESS

Even though the effort made only by 5S implementation leaders and managers could be represented by adapting their evaluation system using scores, such efforts would eventually face a limitation when it came to maintaining true 5S activities across the organization for an extended period of time. They clearly learned that 5S activities could not be maintained without the full-fledged participation of their staff. More importantly, cultivating a higher level of motivation and a sense of collective organizational spirit among the staff was essential. It required a great deal of energy and resources to overcome the challenge of getting their staff to fully understand that the true purpose of performing 5S activities was not for scoring higher points on an evaluation but was for improving our operational productivity and preventing any types of medical accidents from occurring in the first place. Conducting study sessions was extremely effective for establishing a mutual understanding in this respect.

The introduction of a 3-phase evaluation system on a monthly basis allowed for monitoring the status of implementation activities at all times and to maintain the full-participation of the staff. They also learned that it was extremely significant to integrate the opinions of team members in the process of formulating goals and establishing mutual understandings. They tried not to force decisions and biases upon their staff.

With this type of framework, they were able to witness results, which were being fed directly back to managers, for seeking continuous improvement ideas and identifying new objectives for the next month.

12-1-4 FINAL RESULTS

Evaluation scores for each year in this department are as follows:

Year	Score	Grade
1st Year	40 pt	D
2nd Year	65 pt	B
3rd Year	80 pt	A
4th Year	88 pt	AA

★ Score based out of 100 points

Table 12.1 Final Evaluation Scores

12-2 CASE STUDY: UROLOGY OUTPATIENT NURSING DEPARTMENT

12-2-1 CONDITION AND ISSUES PRIOR TO 5S IMPLEMENTATION

The following are examples of conditions and issues that the department was dealing with before implementing 5S.

1) Because the initial "Sort" and "Set in Order" activities failed to yield efficiency in sorting and setting items in order, in many cases a staff member had to borrow certain items from another examination room, as the items in their examination room were unevenly stocked. An efficient use of available treatment time was also not possible as, for example, staff often took a long time to explain to patients the position that they had to take for receiving a prostate examination.

2) Management of medical supplies had much to be desired. For example, staff members realized a shortage of catheters while preparing for a treatment and placed restocking orders immediately after. Sometimes certain items were overstocked and in the way of other supplies, preventing the staff from working efficiently.

3) The door to the outpatient department would close if the stopper was accidentally removed. Patients with an anesthetized shoulder were often hurt by attempting to open the door. Also, the waiting room for patients in wheelchairs could use more space, as it was relatively cramped for its size.

4) Walls in the patient waiting room were plastered with notices, such as announcements and the schedules of doctors, and the furniture used in the room were neither "Sorted" nor "Standardized." Waiting patients did not feel comfortable being in this room for a long period of time.

5) As the availability of storage space in the urology outpatient department was limited, our staff stored some boxes that contained changes of nurse uniforms and stoma supplies under the beds.

6) Walls in the area where a public phone was located became dirty as many memos and phone lists were placed there.

7) Awareness toward "Sort" and "Standardize" among the staff was not unified, therefore 5S was not implemented in a thorough manner.

12-2-2 ACTIVITY PROGRESS

The staff members who had gone through an intensive workshop of mine on "Sort," "Set in Order," and "Shine," shared their new knowledge with colleagues in their workplace. This allowed the entire staff to establish the same awareness that the "true objective of 5S activities is to create a solid foundation for increasing operational efficiency and preventing medical malpractices," and the staff initiated their implementation actions based on this collective commitment.

1. "SORT"

We created a comprehensive "Sort" execution plan, according to the correctly determined implementation procedures for "Sort," and designated responsibilities among staff members. Items were Red Tagged, based on the guidelines for disposing of items, so that unnecessary items were isolated. We finally got rid of many ambiguous items that they had previously been unable to decide what to do with, such as old medical dictionaries, reference literatures, unused manuals, old medical equipment, and unused items in desk drawers. As a result we were able to create additional space, which was made available for introducing efficiency within the outpatient area.

2. "SET IN ORDER"

In order to meet their goal of retrieving necessary items within 30 seconds, placement locations were designated for each item and it was decided upon exactly how it needed to be placed. We also put clear identification on everything so that the items were put back in their designated locations at all times.

- Locations of desks and drawers containing instruction sheets for surgeries were unified in examination rooms #1–#4. A photograph showing the necessary posture for receiving a prostate exam was put on the wall next to the diagnostic table, along with surgery gloves and lubricants, placed in fixed locations nearby. In addition, diagrams that explained the nature and procedures of each surgery were posted in front of the desk so that doctors were able to explain the information to patients in a productive way.

- We applied our continuous improvement ideas to adapting a more efficient method of storing the wide range of catheters that we were using. We designated placement locations for each box containing a certain type of catheter, according to its frequency of use, and each box was color coded and labeled with the name, size, and fixed quantity of contained catheters.

- We created an information board in the waiting room and allowed announcements and notices to be put on the board only. Phone directories that had been placed on the walls near the public phone were completely removed and the phone itself was programmed with the directory information. We also upholstered the furniture in the waiting room in blue, which gave a more pleasant look to the room and increased our patient's satisfaction with the hospital.

- Each storage shelf was colored in either yellow or blue and the way they were all labeled was unified. This allowed for easy identification of the shelves by every staff member. Hospital supplies were easily managed by utilizing the inventory management lists that our staff had created, which allowed them to quickly learn the amount of requested laundry and returned items for daily supplies, such as bed-covers and curtains.

- Boxes that had been used to store nurse uniforms and stoma supplies under the beds were given casters so that they could be easily transported in and out of the treatment rooms. We avoided boxes placed directly on the floors.

- Supplies of necessary medical forms were made clear and restocking orders were made at the predetermined point of remaining volumes. This prevented the operation from stopping at all for a shortage of certain medical forms.

3. "SHINE"

We focused our cleaning effort upon the areas determined to be dirty by putting ourselves in the shoes of our patients and customers. We also acknowledged the need for targeting our continuous improvement measures toward repairing specific defective areas and clearly identified the responsibilities for each staff member to get the job done in a timely manner.

- We created the 5S activity calendar, in which "Shine" activities were clearly indicated as a part of the necessary tasks defined in the daily 5S activity schedule.

- The entrance door was changed to a sliding door and shutters were installed at the reception desk. This improvement eliminated the issue where patients with shoulder anesthesia and elderly patients would get injured by opening the cumbersome doors, as well as provided more space for patients in wheelchairs. This also created an open atmosphere around the reception area and allowed the staff to interact with patients at a much higher level of efficiency.

- We switched from using file cabinets to file shelves so that items, such as various passes and treatment schedule charts used at the time of patients' admittance, could be retrieved much more easily. File shelves were divided into sections labeled, such as "Operation Room," "ESWL Room," "Lumbar Spine Anesthesia," and were color coded according to these unique classifications in order to boost the efficiency of doctors who make the orders for necessary medical treatment to be executed. We also implemented the Kanban System, of the Toyota Production System, for ordering reprints of forms in a timely manner.

12-2-3 LESSONS LEARNED FROM IMPLEMENTATION PROCESS

- Based on our unified theme, "Striving for a Sustainable Environment," our outpatient department has continued to implement the "Standardize" concept in our workplace through leveraging our creative ideas so that recycled items, such as empty supply boxes, empty bottles of saline, and used MRI sand bags, were reutilized in our operations in an absolute manner. We also made use of the items that had been Red Tagged as unnecessary items in other departments in the past.

- The biggest challenge of all was that we first needed to gather a sufficient amount of recycled supplies to be used for administering our 5S ideas. Recycled items were often used as effective communication tools for repeated orders and requests; these are written on items such as wooden sticks. The biggest advantage of this is that such sticks were prepared beforehand, according to the types of orders and requests, so that they did not need to be created each time that a new order or request was released. This is also a great example of how we began applying our creativity to reuse items that could have easily been thrown away in order to increase work efficiency. However, the use of such tools supported by recycled items has been replaced by the implementation of electronic patient charts in recent years.

- We covered ordinary cardboard boxes with used MRI bags (blue) to create "Blue Storage." Then, the boxes were cut into specific dimensions based on the items to be stored and were secured to the floor by applying adhesive tape. The staff in charge of preparing these boxes appeared to have had a hard time in allocating their work time, but effectively managed to spare 5-10 minutes of their daily work time for accomplishing the task.

12-2-4 FINAL RESULTS

- Operational efficiency in our department has drastically improved since we were able to apply "Sort" and "Set in Order" concepts in a way that items and places, such as file shelves, supply storage cabinets, and examination rooms, could be utilized in the most functional and efficient manner.

- Reimbursement costs of disposable medical and office supplies have drastically decreased by managing supplies of goods while pursuing 5S.

- We were successful in unifying the awareness toward "Sort" and "Set in Order" among our staff in the department. As we have continued to persistently practice 5S with the slogan "A More Beautiful, Convenient, and Functional Hospital," our patients began complimenting our efforts and expressed that they felt much more comfortable and safer in our outpatient department than before.

Overview of Supply Division Spending

Year 2004

	Jan.	Feb.	March	April	May	June
Medical Examination Supplies	122,487	110,912	154,915	150,592	150,925	128,661
Medical Consumables	5,180	3,680	3,220	4,230	4,120	7,800
Office Supplies	0	7,664	6,525	7,606	6,170	0
General Hospital Consumables	1,760	12,073	14,125	4,000	1,628	6,863

	July	Aug.	Sept.	Oct.	Nov.	Dec.	Total
Medical Examination Supplies	149,529	139,869					1,107,890
Medical Consumables	5,180	6,800					40,210
Office Supplies	3,568	5,325					36,858
General Hospital Consumables	3,010	5,815					39,274

Year 2003

	Jan.	Feb.	March	April	May	June
Medical Examination Supplies	120,249	141,000	170,143	146,767	175,082	234,740
Medical Consumables	3,680	3,720	6,740	5,180	4,180	4,180
Office Supplies	2,530	476	0	776	11,052	12,288
General Hospital Consumables	12,289	4,025	4,430	6,732	3,212	4,535

	July	Aug.	Sept.	Oct.	Nov.	Dec.	Total
Medical Examination Supplies	136,248	234,946	135,216	121,914	116,885	153,713	1,886,903
Medical Consumables	7,800	5,120	7,360	41,855	4,120	5,180	61,961
Office Supplies	3,210	9,810	1,142	776	1,524	3,298	47,961
General Hospital Consumables	8,039	8,616	4,991	4,826	4,415	41,235	107,345

Figure 12.3 Overview of Supply Division Spending

12-3 CASE STUDY: CHALLENGES OF A 5S LEADER

12-3-1 A 5S LEADER FACING A DEAD-END

A 5S implementation leader, Mr. Takahashi, felt like he had reached a deadlock in implementing 5S on the organizational level after having tried 5S activities with his team members for 3 months. Progress made by other teams instructed by his colleagues was far better than that of his team and all other workplaces began enjoying substantial improvements in operational efficiency. He also learned that the interest level of his team members in practicing 5S has declined significantly compared to how they were at the beginning stage.

Mr. Takahashi truly believed that no matter how hard he had tried to accomplish the 5S objectives, his team members were not motivated to work closely with him to meet his expectations. On the other hand, his team members had attitudes believing that 5S leaders were fully responsible for organizing and executing activities and that they ought to simply follow the instructions given by their leader.

Mr. Takahashi realized that something had to be changed immediately and decided to try harder at promoting the benefits of 5S to his team members. In morning meetings he asked his team members, in a pleading manner, to become more proactively involved in implementing 5S. He continued to do so for the next 3 morning meetings, but found no change of attitude among his team members. He began to understand that his position as a 5S implementation leader simply was not respected and was ignored by the whole team.

12-3-2 GAINING SUPPORT FROM SUPERVISORS

FACTORY TOUR AS A BREAKTHROUGH APPROACH TO SOLVING PROBLEMS

Mr. Takahashi consulted with his supervisors and staff from other departments to derive a solution to his issue. He received the useful recommendation to tour a specific manufacturing plant, where 5S was being implemented throughout the factory, as well as its parent organization.

Mr. Takahashi decided to participate in touring the factory soon after receiving the recommendation. He was first shown around the shop floors of the factory and the managing supervisors of each department explained to him the essence of their 5S activities and implementation challenges, along with some valuable know-how that any 5S leader ought to understand in order to lead 5S implementation in an effective manner. After the tour, Mr. Takahashi continued receiving training and useful information on becoming a better 5S leader by the 5S implementation administration office in the hospital.

Mr. Takahashi learned a great deal of new knowledge from his factory tour experience. He was especially moved by witnessing their 5S leaders, who appeared extremely lively on the shop floor. Even though Mr. Takahashi had just started his responsibility as a 5S leader, he criticized himself for not having this same level of positive attitude and enthusiasm toward his own work.

What the 5S implementation administration office taught Mr. Takahashi was how each 5S leader ought to manage his team members. He had done nothing beyond simply asking his team members to cooperate in the effort, instead of managing the progress that each member had made in an effective manner. He finally realized that his most important responsibilities in implementing 5S was to first establish certain rules for achieving the ideal state of their own workplace and then to formulate effective strategies to meet the objectives, as well as following up with implementation progress and results in a precise manner.

12-3-3 A Persuaded Workforce

After having gained new knowledge and understanding from the factory tour and training experiences, Mr. Takahashi returned to his workplace and began executing his new plans for 5S implementation. He started by explaining to his team members, in detail, what he had learned through the experience. The team members did not actively listen in at first, however, after observing Mr. Takahashi's enthusiasm and passion in his speech, team members started paying closer attention to their 5S leader.

Next, Mr. Takahashi decided to review the existing rules to redefine the ideal state of his workplace. In the past he often imposed his opinions upon such decision making processes.

This time around, however, he made sure that the opinions of his team members were incorporated in the process, which promoted the full-fledged participation of his whole team. For the rules that were enforced on an organizational level, Mr. Takahashi made sure that his team members clearly understood the true purpose behind each rule.

Then Mr. Takahashi decided to make clearly understood the responsibilities assigned to each team member, as their responsibilities had been ambiguous on a practical level in the past. It was not clear before who was in charge of what areas, therefore Mr. Takahashi decided that one staff member alone would be responsible for one specific target area, in order to prevent workers from shifting over responsibilities amongst themselves in a case where more than one staff member was assigned to the same target area.

Last but not least, Mr. Takahashi's team formulated a plan of execution in order to implement 5S in a practical manner. He realized that the plans created in the past had always failed to accommodate the unique requirements of his workplace and therefore appeared irrelevant. He made sure that a plan of execution from that point forward would incorporate the opinions of his team members and to be supported by their consent.

Having utilized these effective approaches, Mr. Takahashi began gaining a greater deal of support and seriousness from his team members in practicing 5S, and made a quantum leap in improving the execution rate of necessary implementation activities in his team. Mr. Takahashi found it surprising that his team members became much more ambitious toward achieving better results as the execution rate continued to improve over time.

A few of the team members went above and beyond and carried out some positive actions, even though such actions were not included in the plan. Mr. Takahashi's team had suffered from some serious challenges in the beginning, but was able to receive the evaluation score of "A" at the second audit. Due to the many changes Mr. Takahashi had made promoting 5S implementation they have continued to accomplish greater results to the present day.

12-3-4 LESSONS LEARNED BY THE 5S LEADER

The 5S leader, Mr. Takahashi, learned much through having lead and managed 5S activities. He learned how to identify true objectives at any stages of 5S implementation and how to internalize what is required to be able to manage his team members effectively. He also acknowledged that the ultimate objective of 5S was not simply to make a workplace appear clean and organized, but it was to improve the efficiency and safety of hospital operations by organizing various processes of work in an orderly manner, as well as his team's collective approach toward work itself.

Mr. Takahashi believes now that the implementation of 5S equals the way work is performed on a daily basis. He keeps in mind at all times the significance of the PDCA management cycle approach, which involves key actions in 5S implementation process: "Plan," "Do," "Check," and "Act." Mr. Takahashi was also taught the necessity of providing not ambiguous, but clear and precise directions to his team members. He realized that his instructions may have been clear to himself but in many cases may have been imprecise to his team members.

CHAPTER 13
LOOKING INTO THE FUTURE

13-1 VIRTUES AND EFFECTIVENESS OF CLINICAL 5S REGARDING THE ENTIRE HOSPITAL

THE FOLLOWING ASPECTS OF 5S can be summarized in order to explain why 5S activities are effective in a hospital environment:

- The positive outcome of 5S is tangible and can be attained in a short period of time
- Many hospitals have not yet adapted "Sort" and "Set in Order" concepts in their operations, which makes it easier for such hospitals to appreciate positive and immediate results upon implementing 5S
- It has been my experience that women appear to be more natural at performing 5S than men, which makes implementing 5S thoroughly in hospitals easier as they generally employ more women than men

13-1-1 TRYING NEW THINGS

Takeda General Hospital has been provided with many new things to try since introducing various incentive projects for implementing 5S in a more absolute manner. Trying new things may seem like an easy thing to do, however it often requires detailed justification for choosing a certain decision over another and has to overcome any resistance to accommodating new changes in a workplace.

The question here is why we decided to promote new changes while knowing that such serious challenges and risks existed within the organization. The answer is that it was feared the employers may have felt a diminished sense of reward toward attaining positive results because the hospital had fallen into a rut in practicing 5S.

Everyone was aware of what a versatile tool 5S is and that they should not depend upon some evaluation system by a third party to oversee the progress of 5S implementation. They wanted to take advantage of the versatility of 5S to keep their staff motivated and dedicated to trying new things, whether they succeeded or failed. The followings are some examples.

1. TRYING NEW THINGS IN TERMS OF "AUTHORITY"

- Transferring authority from head nurse/section manger to team leader/group leader

Team leaders and group leaders were given full authority to oversee 5S implementation within targeted areas and received a series of customized workshop training programs for their special needs and skill levels. This allowed 5S activities to target real issues by remaining in close contact with the staff in a workplace.

2. TRYING NEW THINGS IN TERMS OF "ITEMS"

- Transferring authority to each workplace so that the final treatment of unnecessary items was decided on a workplace level

By allowing each workplace to make their own decisions about disposing of items, without referring to the opinions of the purchasing department, we were able to eliminate a number of medical equipment items that had been left abandoned for a long time. 20 digital cameras were then purchased and they had their staff members document the actual cases of "Sort" practices they had conducted. Comparing such case study materials allowed us to easily make correct decisions for subsequent cases, and the entire process was an effective method of teaching the essence of the PDCA cycle to our staff members.

3. Trying new things in terms of "financial support"

- $30 was provided for each 5S implementation as a reserve fund to prepare for "Set in Order" activities

The money was given for the purpose of ensuring the sense of independence and unique creativity of each workplace in executing various 5S activities. Even though some workplaces complained about the amount being too low in the beginning, they made up for it by effectively utilizing recycled materials and began finding the true value in applying their creative ideas in order to gain a higher level of uniqueness in their 5S implementation techniques.

4. Trying new things in terms of "sharing information"

- Information exchange meetings were held frequently to share excellent implementation ideas among staff members

Useful information related to various 5S activities were shared via the intranet, email systems, and corporate newsletters, for the purpose of eliminating the gap among each workplace's access to information.

13-1-2 Direct Benefits of Clinical 5S

The followings describe some examples of direct benefits of Clinical 5S in detail.

1. Elimination of waste in searching for items.

   Implementing 5S in an absolute manner has eliminated the wasteful searching for necessary items, such as looking for medical charts and prescriptions in a nurse center, and locating documents in the administrative department. These improvements have allowed staff members to be able to concentrate more of their energy and resources on solving the issues of patients.

2. Efficient use of available working space.

   There are many mixes of items, such as medicines, medical equipment, and documents in a hospital environment. It is predicted that the tendency of having to accommodate a wide range of items will continue as our medical practices keep improving to a higher level of sophistication over time. Therefore it is extremely critical that such items are placed in the most functional and efficient manners, in order to accommodate medical advancements, since the available space in our hospital wards are limited.

   5S kept calling for a continuous improvement effort and allowed the hospital to maximize the use of available workspace by providing clear guidelines for deciding to either dispose of items or appropriate items to other departments, so that they could be reused for other purposes.

3. Reduction of human errors.

   Implementing 5S thoroughly has built a solid foundation for preventing human errors from occurring in hospital operations. In particular, the use of "Visual Management" has allowed the detection of risks by sight, which is extremely critical to human error risk management.

4. Prevention of accidents within the hospital.

   Hospitals are always required to accommodate people who are weak, both mentally and physically, at all times. Therefore, it is extremely important to create an environment in which such people feel comfortable and safe when they visit your hospital. To achieve this purpose we need to be committed to continuous improvement efforts, such as maintaining clear passageways in the hospital, clarifying information signs, eliminating dangerous areas, and so on, through conducting various 5S activities.

5. Increased level of satisfaction among patients and visitors.

It is important for our valued patients and customers to feel that they are getting the best treatment they deserve when visiting the hospital. Having this philosophy in mind at all times, and building a hospital environment around it, will lead to establishing an increased level of satisfaction among patients and customers. The patients of Takeda General Hospital will now always enjoy a sense of cleanliness in their rooms and have hospital information indicated in a clear manner. All of these positive effects are attributed to Clinical 5S implementation.

13-2 FUTURE PLANS FOR CLINICAL 5S IMPLEMENTATION

As represented by the DPC system, which stands for "Diagnosis," "Procedure," "Combination" (a.k.a. DRG 'Diagnostic Related Group'), hospitals will have to pay closer attention to how they can level the quality of services while reducing the overall operational costs from now on. The most effective method of achieving this purpose is to create operational standards and specifications and analyze the cause of deviant cases, then incorporate our findings into overcoming our future challenges.

In this sense, the creation of standardization and operational manuals is extremely important. As far as our personal 5S activities are concerned, we created an Execution Planning Manual for "Set in Order" and a Standard Procedure Manual for "Shine" to serve that purpose. We understood that the content of such manuals could be effective only when the involvement of sufficient interested parties are present during the process of creating the manuals. Even more, if we struggle to collect the necessary information, we will most likely fail to have the actual place of work accommodate the manuals in a timely manner to ensure positive results.

Our present and future challenge is having staff members understand the true meaning of such standardization and operation manuals, which will facilitate the manuals being shared with anyone easily. That also leads to continuously collecting empirical data for future analysis, which is extremely similar to the challenge that we have overcome for implementing 5S activities. Therefore, our plan is to gradually transition from focusing on promoting Visual Management, as well as the management of items and the workplace through conducting 5S activities, to applying 5S concepts to the content of our operation in order to execute much more efficient ways of completing our operations on a daily basis.

13-3 FUTURE CHALLENGES OF CLINICAL 5S IMPLEMENTATION

As I have explained, establishing appropriate 5S standards and practical manuals is extremely effective for ensuring a successful implementation of Clinical 5S. However, as this is only a preparation stage, it can be problematic since much time has to be spent on first establishing the guidelines. It cannot be said that this type of time-consuming process is the most desirable tool for our decision-making process, given the fact that our medical working environment continues to have to accommodate fast-pace changes on a daily basis.

Our future goals are to train our workers to be able to choose their own actions, based on what they judge will be the best and highest-quality care for our customers and patients. Until each staff member becomes independent and capable of proactively participating in their own decision making, we will continue to implement Clinical 5S and establish a desirable organizational culture for the long term.

TEMPLATES

TEMPLATES OF THE FORMS AND LETTERS USED
BY TAKEDA GENERAL HOSPITAL DURING THEIR
5S IMPLEMENTATION

Takeda General Hospital
5S "Sort" Schedule

5S "Sort" Implementation Leader Training

First - 6/25/2001
Second - 7/2/2001
Third - 7/3/2001
Fourth - 7/26/2001

Takeda General Hospital 5S "Kick-off" Declaration
by Kobato Committee Chairman
(announcement during the morning meeting)

8/1 Wed.

(1)   Submission deadline for "Sort" Action Plans — 8/10 Fri.

(2)   Last day of photographing for "Sort" analysis — 8/16 Thur.

(3)   Red Tagging across the organization — 8/30 Thur.- 9/6 Thur.

(4)   Finalizing listing of unnecessary items — 8/30 Thur.- 9/6 Thur.

(5)   Disposal of unnecessary items across the organization — 8/17 Fri.- 9/7 Fri.

(6)   Assessment for the lists of unnecessary items
        (Nursing Dept., Administration Dept., CM Dept.) — 9/10 Mon.- 9/14 Fri.

(7)   Transferring unnecessary items to temporary storage areas — 9/17 Mon.- 9/21 Fri.

(8)   The last day for "Sort" implementation — 9/14 Fri.

Takeda General Hospital
5S "Sort" Action Plan Gantt Chart (Idea)

Action		Year 2001														
		June		July			August			September			
		20	30	10	20	30	10	20	30	10	20	30	
	Training for 5S "Sort" Implementation Leaders	6/25											
	Takeda General Hospital 5S kick-off declaration					8/1							
(1)	Submission deadline for "Sort" Action Plan			7/2 - 7/3	7/26		8/10						
(2)	Last day of photographing for "Sort" analysis							8/16					
(3)	Red Tagging across the organization								8/30 - 9/6				
(4)	Finalizing listing of unnecessary items								8/30 - 9/6				
(5)	Disposal of unnecessary items across the organization								8/17 - 9/7				
(6)	Assessment for the lists of unnecessary items									9/10 - 9/14			
(7)	Transporting unnecessary items to Temporary storage space									9/17 - 9/21			
(8)	Last day for "Sort" implementation									9/14			

177

Takeda General Hospital
"Sort" Action Plans (Idea)

No. _____

Target Area Department	Leader	Manager

Department _____
Section/Division/Ward _____
Team _____

No.	"Sort" Target Area		Schedule							Main Implementer	Assessment Dates made by Main Implementer		Assessment Date
			1st Month		2nd Month		3rd Month						Assessor
1.		Plan									Month/Date	Month/Date	Month/Date
		Actual											
2.		Plan									Month/Date	Month/Date	Month/Date
		Actual											
3.		Plan									Month/Date	Month/Date	Month/Date
		Actual											
4.		Plan									Month/Date	Month/Date	Month/Date
		Actual											
5.		Plan									Month/Date	Month/Date	Month/Date
		Actual											
6.		Plan									Month/Date	Month/Date	Month/Date
		Actual											
7.		Plan									Month/Date	Month/Date	Month/Date
		Actual											

Takeda General Hospital
"Sort" Standard Guidelines (Idea)

"Sort" item		Red Tagging Duration	Actions to take after Red Tagging Duration Expires	
Target	Classification			
Patient Charts		Exempt		
Xray Films		Exempt		
Medical Examination Supplies	Medical Consumables	Within 6 months or Specific Deadlines	Disposal decision to be made with Medical Supply Advisory Board. For expensive items, submit an application for final decisions.	
	Medical Consumables Supply			
	Medical Materials			
Medical Devices	Medical Devices	6 months	Leased Items	Follow the Disposal Rules for Under-Utilized Items
Medical Equipment	Beddings, etc.		Financial Control/ Number Controlled Items	Follow the Retirement Rules for Under-Utilized Items
Fixtures and Furniture	Desks/Chairs Shelves/Lockers Filing Cabinets etc.		Business Expense Items	Disposal or Reuse in other Departments
Literature	Original Documents	6 Months	Common Documents	Manage by Document Storage Standards
			Personal Documents	Dispose when Final Documents are Completed
	Receipts		Common Documents	Manage by Document Storage Standards
			Personal Documents	Convert into Common Files
	Manuals		Common Documents	Setting Due Dates/ Dispose of Unsolicited Documents
			Personal Documents	Convert into Common Documents

★ Avoid copied documents for individual use - share the originals.

Takeda General Hospital
5S "Set in Order" Implementation Action Plan

● 5S Implementation Leader Training (Set in Order)	First - 10/2/2001
Instructor: Akio Takahara from Basic Management Laboratory	Second - 10/3/2001 Third - 10/15/2001 Fourth - 10/16/2001

● "Set in Order" kick-off declaration by Kobato Committee Chairman (Morning Meeting)	10/17 Wed.

(1) "Set in Order" workplace meetings — 10/17 Wed. - 10/31 Wed.

(2) Due date for submission of "Set in Order" action plan (After submission, each workplace initiate its own "Set in Order" action plan) — 10/31 Wed.

(3) Financial aid for 5S "Set in Order" preparation starts (Planned) — 11/1 Thur. - 1/31 Thur.

(4) The last day for photography for "Set in Order" assessment — 11/7 Wed.

(5) End-of-the-year comprehensive cleaning period (Repeat "Sort") — 12/11 Mon. - 12/28 Fri.

(6) Finishing date for preliminary "Set in Order" implementation — 2/22/2002 Mon.

(7) "Set in Order" assessment week by instructor Takahara — 2/25/2002 Mon. - 3/1/2002 Fri.

(8) Announcement of "Set in Order" assessment and results — 3/20/2002 Tues.

(9) ● Announcement for "Sort & Set in Order" goals for the next year — 3/27/2002 Wed.
    ● Awarding ceremony for departments with the highest 5S achievement for 2001

Kobato Committee Chairman
(Morning Meeting)

Common "Set in Order" Rules for Takeda General Hospital

5S Implementation Committee

For implementing Set in Order, the following requirements have to be met at all times:
1. Placement location is clearly identified for each item.
2. Items are placed as they should be.
3. Information is clearly displayed according to the rules.

1) Floor
Placement is marked by tape on the floor, then name labels are attached to the floor for each item
Rule: Green vinyl tape (width: 19mm) must be used. (refer to diagram #1)

2) Shelves and cabinets (refer to diagram #2)
1. Shelf/cabinet name tag is placed on upper left corner
2. Name of the person in charge of maintenance is attached on the upper right corner
3. Name label for each item is attached below the corresponding item
4. Items are placed with older items (older dates) closer to the retrieving point and newer items (newer dates) behind older items
(The Tepra Tape to be used here has to be white and 12mm width. Font color is black.)
5. File folders must be placed according to a given sequence (ABC, dates, 123.. etc.)
6. Each document must be given a title and filed in folders in an upright position

3) Work tables, office desks, and counters
1. Do not leave anything on the desk after work is done
2. Placement is partitioned by marking tape and name label is attached to placement for each item
3. Indicate the name of the person in charge of managing
4. Do not put any items under office desks

4) Others
1. For electric wires and such, bundle them up so that they do not touch the floor
2. Line up documents in designated locations on a bulletin board
3. Avoid overlapping documents on a bulletin board
4. Identify expiration dates for documents posted on a bulletin board
5. Do not place any random items on shelves and cabinets

Diagram #1					
Item to be Surrounded	Color	Width	Display Material	Display Method	Target Items
	Green	Width 19mm (Determined by Supply Department)	Vinyl Tape	To be displayed within the Tape Width	- Items to be placed on the floor - Items to be used after being transported Ex: Carts, Lifts, Pallets, Storage Boxes, Inspection Boxes, Medical Supplies, Components, Defective Items, etc.

Diagram 1:
Standardizing the display of fixed placement locations

Fixed locations have to be indicated for:
1. Items whose placement boundaries are marked and that are stored at a specific location.
2. For each placement location, it should be labeled as "oxoxox location".

Continuous Improvement Idea Diagram (Diagram #2)

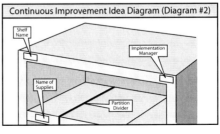

5S Implementation: "Sort" Guidelines
October 2001 - March 2002

October 17, 2001

Dear Implementation Leaders,

Introduction

We have decided to implement "Set in Order" as a part of our organization-wide 5S implementation. "Set in Order" is a fundamental principle of 5S activities and we have made a strong commitment to continuously implement it on a one year basis. As we are just starting out, please do not get stressed out over it. Instead, begin by getting a feel for "Set in Order", as it is most important to be able to continue our efforts over a long period of time.

There are many tools that can be used for executing the ideas behind "Straighten." For this period the Implementation Committee has prepared Tepra Tape and other useful marking tapes. We will purchase more tools as necessary, however please attempt to practice "Straighten" with existing tools by utilizing your craftiness and creativity.

We are, however, considering providing up to 3,000 Yen per "Set in Order" Implementation Action Plan for consumable supplies, other than Tepra Tape and marking tapes, which can be effectively used for indicating "placement location", "placement method", and "placement labels". For details, please refer to the document titled "5S Set in Order Preparation Budget".

As well, we are planning on awarding selected workplaces that have achieved the best 5S results after assessing the progress for the next 6 months.

We wish you the best in implementing "Set in Order".

Procedures for Implementing "Set in Order"

1. Define your Responsibilities
   Reconfirm your scope of responsibilities for practicing "Set in Order". Fundamentally, your responsibilities remain the same as for "Sort".

2. Maintain Open Communication with your Subordinates
   Provide clear explanations to your subordinates about the true objectives and Action Plans for implementing "Set in Order" this time around.

   Make sure that your subordinates have a clear understanding for the common implementation rules. If such rules are still not in place, have them establish a set of common rules that best fit their unique working environment. The most important thing is to establish a work atmosphere where each staff member is willing to cooperate with one another for achieving "Set in Order" objectives.

3. Create "Set in Order" Action Plans
   Identify "Set in Order" target areas and create Action Plans while designating a responsible manager. By referring to "Set in Order" checklists for each target area, identify existing problems with current situations and formulate detailed solutions for each problem at hand. Also consider changing the overall layout for placing items in your work area.

   Keep the original document for the "Set in Order" Action Plan you created and submit a copy to the Business Management Department.

Continued

4. Photograph your Workplace with a Digital Camera

Upon completion of your "Set in Order" Action Plan, start taking photos of each target area in the sequence of your planned actions. A digital camera can be picked up for your use from the Supply Department, as before when "Sort" was put in practice. After completing the photographing, have each photo printed out and maintain them in your workplace.

5. Executing "Set in Order"

As the Action Plan states, initiate implementing "Set in Order" while following the rules after photographing each target area. Apply as many ideas and as much craftiness as your team can, and begin implementation with what you already have access to in your work area.

Determine an appropriate time in which your team should practice "Set in Order". Make sure it is within the working hours, if possible. As we understand that you will still have items to be sorted while implementing "Set in Order", we have set aside some time to refocus on executing "Sort". (December, 10 -28, 2001)

If you discover additional unnecessary items, report them to the Supply Department and attach a Red Tag to each item.

6. Finalize "Set in Order" Implementation and photographing with digital camera

Evaluate how "Set in Order" was practiced by comparing results to the Action Plans. Take photographs of each workplace after the implementation for comparison.

7. Inspecting the progress of "Set in Order" Implementation

Members of the 5S Implementation Committee and instructor Takahara will visit your workplace in order to assess "Set in Order" progress at an appropriate time, on a regular basis. They will assess how closely your team is complying with the rules and the level of creativity that is being put into executing "Set in Order" in your work areas.

We plan to make our assessments available to other departments and will provide awards to the departments that have scored the highest achievements in implementing "Set in Order."

"Set in Order" Inspection Checklist			Day		Month		Year	

Target Area							

Item	No.	Check Item	Score					Comments
"Sort"	1	There are no unnecessary items around target areas or on surrounding floors	5	4	3	2	1	
	2	There are no unnecessary items within target areas	5	4	3	2	1	
	3	Quantity of items is appropriate and not overstocked	5	4	3	2	1	
	4	"Set in Order" is implemented on a regular basis	5	4	3	2	1	
3 Elements of "Set in Order"	5	Placement area for each item is clearly identified	5	4	3	2	1	
	6	Each item is labeled	5	4	3	2	1	
	7	Labels on items can be easily understood	5	4	3	2	1	
	8	Placement areas are clearly partitioned	5	4	3	2	1	
	9	Placement for each item is clearly labeled	5	4	3	2	1	
	10	Placement for each item can easily be understood	5	4	3	2	1	
	11	Labels are not worn off	5	4	3	2	1	
	12	Placement areas follow parallel-perpendicular rules	5	4	3	2	1	
	13	Items are placed in a correct manner (matching with labels)	5	4	3	2	1	
	14	Items are placed in a way that they can be retrieved in the easiest manner	5	4	3	2	1	
	15	Target areas are clearly labeled (such as the names of the shelves)	5	4	3	2	1	
	16	Name of the person responsible for managing 5S implementation is clearly displayed	5	4	3	2	1	
Implementation Method	17	Rules of "Set in Order" are clearly established	5	4	3	2	1	
	18	Full participation towards 5S implementation is always encouraged	5	4	3	2	1	
	19	There are some areas where new ideas and creativity are being implemented	5	4	3	2	1	
	20	The level of implementation progress is in line with targeted achievement	5	4	3	2	1	
Total Score								

List of Unnecessary Items

		Filing Date			
		Filed by (dept.)			
List of Unnecessary Items		Creator	Supply Department		
			Inspector:	Approved by:	

No.	Item Name	Sort No.	Quantity	Storage Duration	Comments
1.					
2.					
3.					
4.					
5.					
6.					
7.					
8.					
9.					
10.					

Akio Takahara

| Continuous Improvement Request Form and Solution Action Report |

Continuous Improvement Request Form for Problem Areas				

No._____

Department		Name		Request Date	

Problem Area	Description		Solution	Person in Charge

- -

| Solution Action Report |

No._____

Problem Area	Person Fixing the Problem	Solution	Date Solution was Applied	Results

Takeda General Hospital:
5S "Sort" & "Shine" Schedule for Year 2004-2005 (first-half)

⊙ Implementation theme for this period ⊙
"Experiencing improvement based on actual documentation (photos)"

● "Sort" and "Shine" Kick-off declaration   4/14/2004 Wed.
by Kobato Committee Chairman (morning meeting)

(1) Workplace Meeting/"Before Straighten" photographing period   4/14 Wed. - 5/21 Fri.

(2) 5S "Shine" training period: May 1 to May 12 (AM & PM)   5/11 Tues. - 5/12 Wed.
Instructor: Akio Takahara

(3) Due date for submitting "Shine" Action Plan - "Shine" begins   5/24 Mon.
Due date for submitting "Set in Order" Action Plan - "Straighten" begins

(4) Accepting requests for 5S "Set in Order" financial aid   7/30 Fri. - 8/13 Fri.

⎡ Applications cannot be accepted ⎤
⎣ after 16:00 on the last day. ⎦

(5) Finish date for 6th "Set in Order" implementation   8/13 Fri.
Last day to take "After Set in Order" photos.
If you have personally taken some photographs, please
bring them to the Business Management Department
to be added to our database.

(6) "Set in Order" inspection by Instructor Takahara (total of 8 days)   8/16 Mon. - 8/31 Tues.

(7) Inspection results announcement (planned)   9/15 Wed.

(8) Award ceremony for departments achieving the best 5S results   9/22 Wed.
for 2004 (first half)

Awarded by Kobato Committee Chairman on Wednesday, September 22 (morning meeting).

About Available Handouts:

☐ Blue handout contains information about "Set in Order"
☐ Yellow handout contains information about "Shine"
☐ White handout contains information related to respective
application procedures and other related information

April 14, 2004

To all Managing staff and General Staff:

Guidelines for "Shine" Target Areas and Cleaning Methods

1. Areas where our third-party building maintenance company is responsible for cleaning is exempt from our "Shine" activities.
   Please refer to the attached floor map. Red areas indicate the area where we are responsible for implementing "Shine." Only those areas are subjected to the inspection to be carried out by instructor Takahara.

2. If an area is utilized only by your workplace then your workplace is responsible for implementing "Sort" in the area.
   Refrain from relying on the building maintenance people. Managers should encourage their staff to take the initiative to participate in cleaning.

3. For commonly-used areas, please share "Shine" responsibilities among departments that utilize such areas.
   (Department/Division Leaders should take a lead in discussions for this matter)

4. Make sure that managers give clear instructions to their staff for "Shine" responsibility sharing and methods of cleaning.

5. Each workplace must create "Shine" standards, based on our requirements, and submit them to the Business Management Department.

6. Notice about "Shine" implementation assessment checklists.
   Every workplace should assess its "Shine" execution based on "Shine" standards by using the attached assessment checklist (monthly/weekly).
   Instructor Takahara may ask to see your assessment checklists when he conducts inspections in August.

To Our General Administrative Staff

We are currently asking for volunteers to perform cleaning; mainly weeding around our buildings. Same as last year, under the approval of the Administration Department Section Managers, we ask the administrative staff to take a leading role in accomplishing this task. Each staff member should be responsible for a certain area, according to our shared responsibility diagram.

Dates of execution should be determined by each workplace and will be shared across the organization via intranet. We have had many staff personnel outside of the Administration Department show interest and participation in this activity.

Even though these areas will be exempt from 5S assessment inspection, we encourage your participation as this is a great opportunity to express our desires towards a higher level of customer satisfaction and our passion towards work itself.

(Our goal: Once or twice a month, for 30 minutes, each staff member should complete the "Shine" and weeding requirements for a particular area.)

What is "Sort?"
1. To maintain a work environment without dirt, trash, and dust.
2. To place each item in their designated locations at all times.
3. To inspect to see if there are any problems, such as ripped labels, while cleaning.

1. Make Clear "Sort" Standards (refer to example #1)
　① "Sort" target area
　② "Sort" method
　③ "Sort" executor
　④ "Sort" implementation checklist (frequency: daily, weekly, monthly, etc)

"Sort" Standards: Example #1

"Sort" Target Area: Medicine Cabinet #1　　　　　　　　"Sort" Executor: ○○○○

Target Area	Frequency	Method	Standard Time
1. Medicine Case Lid	Once a week	Wet Wiping	5 minutes
2. Inside of Medicine Cabinets	Once a month	Wet Wiping/Alcohol Wiping	20 minutes

2. Create a "Sort" Implementation Checklist (refer to example #2 & #3)

Daily "Sort" Checklist: Example #2

Month _____　　　　　　　　　　　　　Checker _____

Day Target Area (Executors Name)	1	2	3	4	5	6	7
Floors in Nurse Stations and Rest Areas							
Sinks in Nurse Stations and Rest Areas							

Weekly "Sort" Checklist: Example #3

Checked in _____ Month _____ Checker _____

Week Target Area (Executors Name)	1st Week	2nd Week	3rd Week	4th Week	5th Week
Areas Around Computers					
Medicine Case Lids					

"Sort" Standardization Sheet

Name of Workplace _____

Manager in Charge _____

"Sort" Target Area _____

"Sort" Executor _____

	Where?	Frequency	Method of "Sort"	Targeted "Sort" Duration
1.				
2.				
3.				
4.				
5.				
6.				
7.				
8.				

Daily "Sort" Activity Checklist

Workplace Name _____

Month _____   Checker _____

Day Target Area (Person in Charge)	1	2	3	4	5	6	7	8	9	10	11	12	13	14	15	16	17	18	19	20	21	22	23	24	25	26	27	28	29	30	31
( ) ( )																															
( ) ( )																															
( ) ( )																															
( ) ( )																															
( ) ( )																															
( ) ( )																															
( ) ( )																															
( ) ( )																															

"Shine" Activity Weekly Check Sheet

Workplace Name _____ Assessment Date _____ Assessor _____

Target Area (Person in Charge) / Week	1st Week	2nd Week	3rd Week	4th Week	5th Week
( ) ( )					
( ) ( )					
( ) ( )					
( ) ( )					
( ) ( )					
( ) ( )					
( ) ( )					
( ) ( )					

PHOTOS

BEFORE AND AFTER PHOTOS TAKEN BY
TAKEDA GENERAL HOSPITAL DURING THEIR
5S IMPLEMENTATION

MAIN BUILDING, 9TH FLOOR, ELEVATOR HALL
(NURSING DEPARTMENT)

Before

After

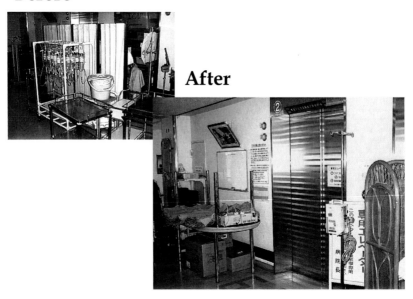

MAIN BUILDING, 9TH FLOOR, REST AREA
(NURSING DEPARTMENT)

Before

After

MAIN BUILDING, 7TH FLOOR, NURSE STATION #1
(NURSING DEPARTMENT)

Before

After

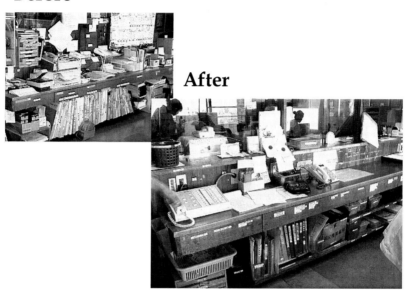

MAIN BUILDING, 7TH FLOOR, NURSE STATION #2
(NURSING DEPARTMENT)

Before

After

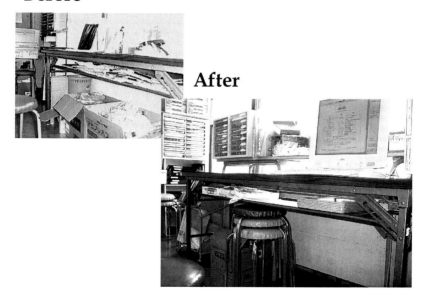

MAIN BUILDING, 7TH FLOOR, AREA AROUND ICE MACHINE
(NURSING DEPARTMENT)

Before

After

MAIN BUILDING, 7TH FLOOR, SUPPLY STORAGE
(NURSING DEPARTMENT)

Before

After

MAIN BUILDING, 5TH FLOOR, NURSE STATION
(NURSING DEPARTMENT)

Before

After

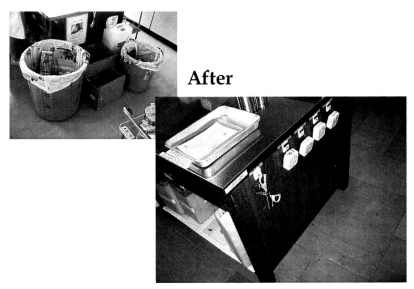

CENTRAL BUILDING #2, 2ND FLOOR, NURSE STATION
(NURSING DEPARTMENT)

Before

After

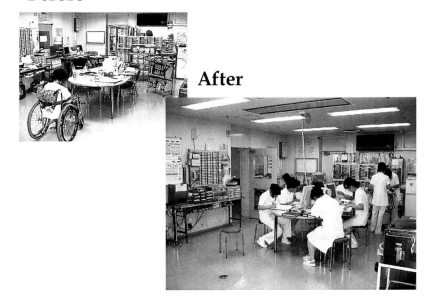

CENTRAL BUILDING #1, 2ND FLOOR, NURSE STATION #1
(NURSING DEPARTMENT)

Before

After

CENTRAL BUILDING #1, 2ND FLOOR, NURSE STATION #2
(NURSING DEPARTMENT)

Before

After

Central Building #1, 2nd Floor, Corridor Area
(Nursing Department)

Before

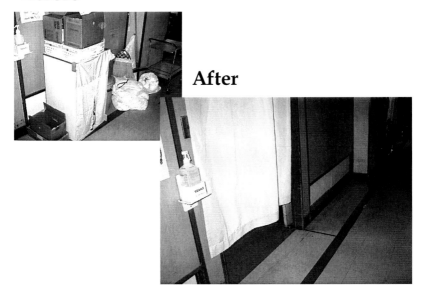

After

Main Building, Underground Floor, Injection Receiving
Window (CM Department)

Before

After

Main Building, Underground Floor, Storage Areas for
I.V. Supplies   (CM Department)

Before

After

Main Building, Underground Floor, Computer Desk,
Pharmacy Office   (CM Department)

Before

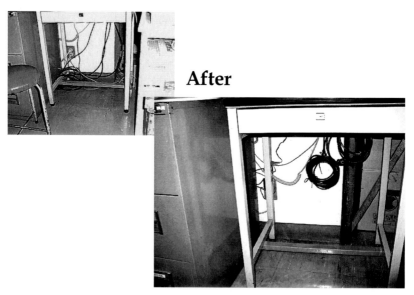

After

MAIN BUILDING, SUPPLY DEPARTMENT/STORAGE SHELVES FOR
CLAIMED ITEMS   (CM DEPARTMENT)

Before

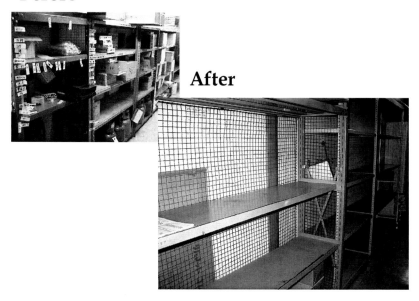

After

MAIN BUILDING, SUPPLY DEPARTMENT/STORAGE SHELVES FOR
ADMINISTRATIVE SUPPLIES   (ADMIN. DEPARTMENT)

Before

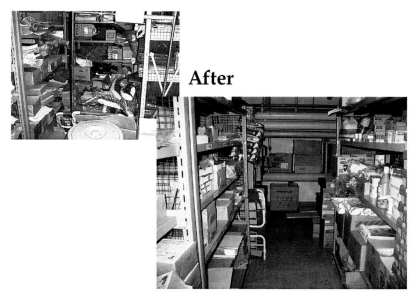

After

MAIN BUILDING, UNDERGROUND FLOOR, SUPPLY/STORAGE
SHELVES FOR ADMINISTRATIVE SUPPLIES #2 (ADMIN. DEPARTMENT)

Before

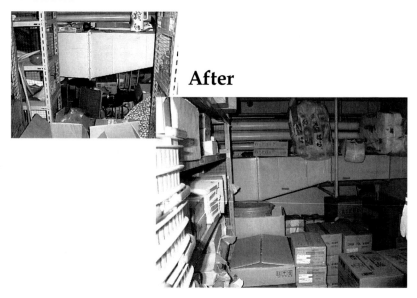

After

MAIN BUILDING, UNDERGROUND FLOOR, SUPPLY/STORAGE
SPACE FOR MEDICAL EXAM SUPPLIES (ADMIN. DEPARTMENT)

Before

After

MEDICAL EXAMINATION IT DEPARTMENT/DESK
(ADMIN. DEPARTMENT)

Before

After

MEDICAL EXAMINATION IT DEPARTMENT/X-RAY FILM STORAGE
(ADMIN. DEPARTMENT)

Before

After

MEDICAL EXAMINATION IT DEPARTMENT/PATIENT CHART STORAGE
(ADMIN. DEPARTMENT)

Before

After

FACILITIES DIVISION/DESK
(ADMIN. DEPARTMENT)

Before

After

FACILITIES DIVISION/SUPPLY STORAGE
(ADMIN. DEPARTMENT)

Before

After

FACILITIES DIVISION/BOILER ROOM
(ADMIN. DEPARTMENT)

Before

After

MAIN BUILDING, UNDERGROUND FLOOR, ELEVATOR HALL
(ADMIN. DEPARTMENT)

Before

After

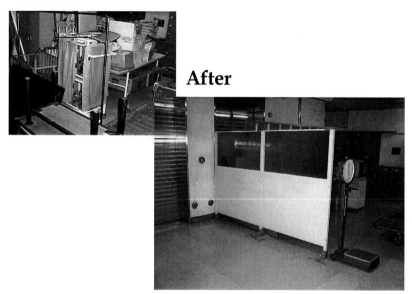

MANAGING NURSE OFFICE/STORAGE AREA
(ADMIN. DEPARTMENT)

Before

After

BUSINESS PROJECT MANAGEMENT DEPARTMENT, BOOK SHELVES
(ADMIN. DEPARTMENT)

Before

After

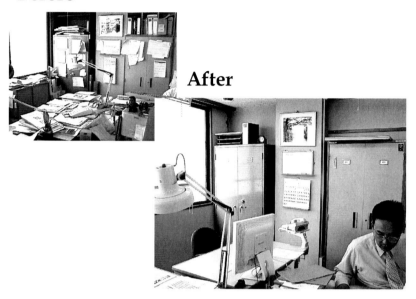

BUSINESS PROJECT MANAGEMENT DEPARTMENT, BOOK SHELVES #2
(ADMIN. DEPARTMENT)

Before

After

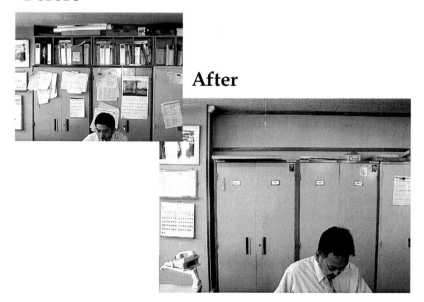

ACCOUNTING DEPARTMENT/FILING CABINET AREA
(ADMIN. DEPARTMENT)

Before

After

ACCOUNTING DEPARTMENT/FILING CABINET DRAWERS
(ADMIN. DEPARTMENT)

Before

After

ADMINISTRATION OFFICE/DESK
(ADMIN. DEPARTMENT)

Before

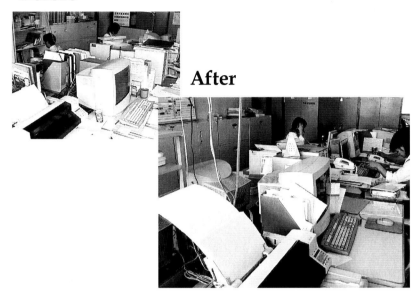

After

ADMINISTRATION OFFICE/SUPPLY STORAGE
(ADMIN. DEPARTMENT)

Before

After

ADMINISTRATION OFFICE/DOCUMENT STORAGE
(ADMIN. DEPARTMENT)

Before

After

ADMINISTRATION OFFICE/PAYCHECK RECORDS STORAGE
(ADMIN. DEPARTMENT)

Before

After

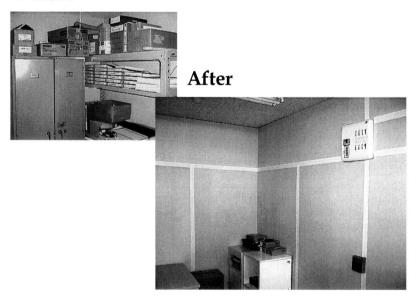

ADMINISTRATION OFFICE/STORAGE ROOM, PRINTER SUPPLIES
(ADMIN. DEPARTMENT)

Before

After

MAIN BUILDING, 5TH FLOOR, NURSE STATION
(NURSING DEPARTMENT)

Before

After

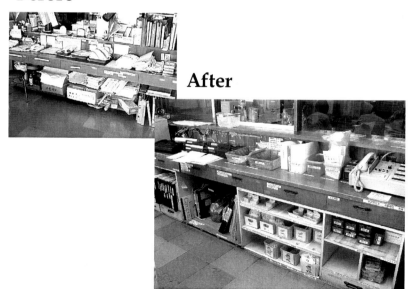

MAIN BUILDING, 5TH FLOOR, SUPPLY STORAGE
(NURSING DEPARTMENT)

Before

After

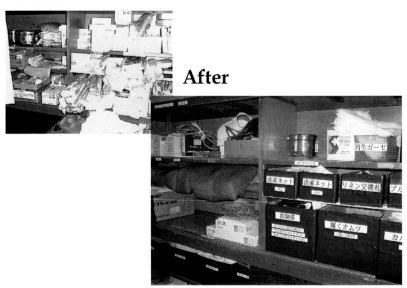

FACILITIES DIVISION / DOCUMENT STORAGE SHELVES
(ADMIN. DEPARTMENT)

Before

After

FACILITIES DIVISION/SUPPLY SHELVES
(ADMIN. DEPARTMENT)

Before

After

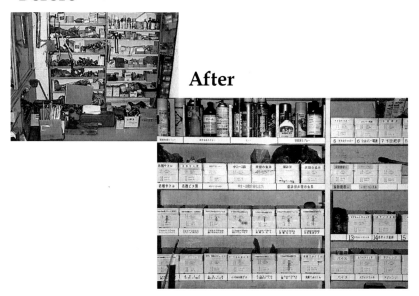

INFORMATION BULLETIN BOARD, NURSING DEPT. CHIEF'S OFFICE
(ADMIN. DEPARTMENT)

Before

After

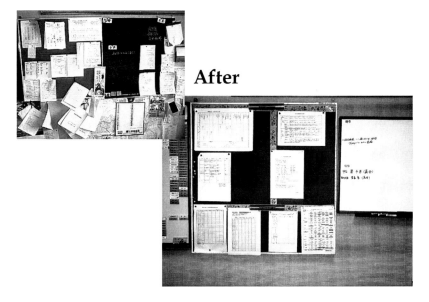

DESK AREA IN DIRECTOR OF NURSING'S OFFICE
(ADMIN. DEPARTMENT)

Before

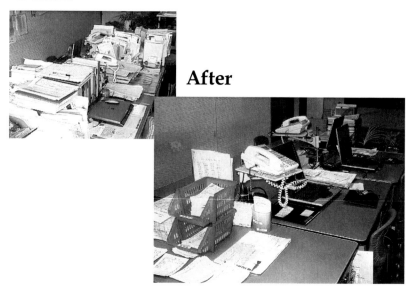

After

LIST OF FIGURES

LIST OF TABLES AND PHOTOS

INDEX

D

I

J

K

L

M

O

T

U

V

W

Publications from Enna

From Enna's new classics by Shigeo Shingo to our Lean Origin Series, Enna provides companies with the foundation of knowledge and practical implementation ideas that will ensure your efforts to internalize process improvement. Reach your vision and mission with the expertise within these world-class texts. Call toll-free (866) 249-7348 or visit us on the web at www.enna.com to order or request our free product catalog.

Fundamental Principles of Lean Manufacturing

Fundamental Principles of Lean Manufacturing is the latest discovered and newly translated classic from Dr. Shigeo Shingo, engineering genius and a driving force behind the successful realization of the Toyota Production System and Lean Manufacturing. This first-time-in-translation book gives modern readers total access to the fundamentals of improving any process. Again, Dr. Shingo amazes and provides you with even more tools to take advantage of in order to solve your problems and pursue a course toward improvement.

ISBN 978-1-897363-07-8 | 2009 | $64.80 | Item: **921**

Mistaken Kanbans

Let Mistaken Kanbans be your roadmap to guide you through the steps necessary to implement and successful Kanban System. This book will help you to not only understand the complexities of a Kanban System but gives you the tools necessary, and the guidance through real-life lessons learned, to avoid disastrous consequences related to the improper use of such systems.

ISBN 978-1-926537-10-8 | 2009 | $27.99 | Item: **919**

The Toyota Mindset

From the brilliant mind of a legend in the LEAN manufacturing world comes the reasoning behind the importance of using your intellect, challenging your workers and why continuous improvement is so important. For anyone who wishes to gain insight into how the Toyota Production System came to be or wants to know more about the person behind TPS this book is a must read!

ISBN 978-1-926537-11-5 | 2009 | $34.99 | Item: **920**

To Order: Enna Corp., 1602 Carolina Street, Unit B3, Bellingham, WA 98229

The Toyota Way in Sales and Marketing

Many companies today are trying to implement the ideas and principles of Lean into non-traditional environments, such as service centers, sales organizations and transactional environments. In this book Mr. Ishizaka provides insight on how to apply Lean operational principles and Kaizen to these dynamic and complicated environments.

ISBN 978-1-926537-08-5 | 2009 | $28.99 | Item: **918**

Organizing for Work

When approached from the Lean perspective, H.L. Gantt's Organizing for Work provides a window into the American origins of the 2nd Pillar of Lean — Respect for People. Gantt, the creator of Gantt charts, galvanized the human aspect of efficiency with razor sharp clarity. Production improvements go astray because we have "ignored the human factor and failed to take advantage of the ability and desire of the ordinary man to learn and improve his position."

ISBN 978-1-897363-80-5 | 2007 | $21.99 | Item: **910**

The Strategos guide to Value Stream & Process Mapping

The Strategos Guide to Value Stream and Process Mapping has proven strategies and helpful tips on facilitating group VSM exercises and puts VSM in the greater Lean context. With photos and examples of related Lean practices, the book focuses on implementing VSM, not just drawing diagrams and graphs.

ISBN 978-1-897363-43-0 | 2007 | $47.00 | Item: **905**

100% Leadership

There is no recipe for success. If there were, we would all use it and it would cease to be effective. Yet, there are many roads that can lead to success. The secret is to choose the right road for your organization among all options. For leaders at all levels, this book provides guidelines for daily decisions and actions, as well as guidance on communication, team-building, planning, and efficiency.

ISBN 978-1-897363-98-0 | 2008 | $21.99 | Item: **915**

Training Materials:
5S Training Package

Our 5S Solution Packages will help your company
create a sustainable 5S program that will turn your
shop floor around and put you ahead of the com-
petition. All of the benefits that come from Lean
Manufacturing are built upon a strong foundation
of 5S. Enna's solution packages will show you how
to implement and sustain an environment of continuous improvement.

Version 1: Sort, Straighten, Sweep, Standardize and Sustain
ISBN 978-0-973750-90-4 | 2005 | $429.99 | Item: 12
Version 2: Sort, Set In Order, Shine, Standardize and Sustain
ISBN 978-1-897363-25-6 | 2006 | $429.99 | Item: 17

Study Mission to Japan

We are excited to present an ex-
clusive trip to the birthplace of
Lean. We provide a one-week
unique tour at a reasonable all-
inclusive price that will guide
you to a better understanding
of Lean Manufacturing principles. Enna has exclusive access
to Toyota and Toyota suppliers due to our publications of Dr. Shigeo Shingo's classic manuscripts. You will have one-on-one access
to Japanese Lean Executives and learn from their experiences and
solutions. We also offer custom private tours for executive management teams over 12 people. Join us on our next tour by visiting www.enna.com/japantrip and register on-line or by telephone
at: +1 (360) 306-5369.

To Order:

Mail orders and checks to:
Enna Products Corporation
ATTN: Order Processing
1602 Carolina Street, Unit B3
Bellingham, WA 98229, USA
Phone: +1 (360) 306-5369 • Fax: (905) 481-0756
Email: info@enna.com

We accept checks and all major credit cards.
Notice: All prices are in US Dollars and are subject to change without notice.